Rod Westfall
10/4/81

CHINA

A Visual Adventure

Carl Mydans
AND
Michael Demarest

Simon and Schuster
New York

OTHER BOOKS BY CARL MYDANS

More Than Meets the Eye
The Violent Peace (with Shelley Mydans)

Copyright © 1979 by Carl Mydans and Michael Demarest
All rights reserved
including the right of reproduction
in whole or in part in any form
Published by Simon and Schuster
A Division of Gulf & Western Corporation
Simon & Schuster Building
Rockefeller Center
1230 Avenue of the Americas
New York, New York 10020

Designed by Stanley S. Drate and Carl Mydans
Manufactured in the United States of America
Printed by The Murray Printing Company
Bound by The Book Press, Inc.
1 2 3 4 5 6 7 8 9 10

Library of Congress Cataloging in Publication Data

Mydans, Carl.
   China, a visual adventure.

   1. China—Description and travel—1976-
2. Mydans, Carl.   I. Demarest, Michael, joint author.
II. Title.
DS712.M9   951.05   79-17262

ISBN 0-671-24946-0

To
Shelley

M.D.
C.M.

Acknowledgments

We are indebted to the many, many interpreters, guides and officials of the China Travel Service (Luxingshe) who cheerfully and tirelessly helped us see and savor China.

Lars-Eric Lindblad, president of Lindblad Travel, the Most Responsible Person on our visit, worked prodigiously to make it a success—and was able to get us visas to China at a time when American journalists were officially not welcomed to the People's Republic.

Allyn Rickett, an old China hand who heads the department of Asian Studies at the University of Pennsylvania, prepared us with invaluable lectures aboard ship, informal interviews on boats, trains, planes, and early-morning walkarounds. Dr. Rickett's former star scholar, Timothy Gelatt, also provided astute interpretation and observation.

Yue Sai-kan, Dr. Sam Rosen and his wife Helen, J. C. Head and George Lang, all of New York City, were generous with advice and insights.

We are particularly grateful to our friends and colleagues at *Time* who facilitated our trip: Managing Editor Ray Cave, Executive Editor Jason McManus and Assistant Business Manager Harriet Watt; correspondents Richard Bernstein, David DeVoss, Bing Wong and Marcia Gauger; and John Durniak, who was the magazine's photographic editor. We are especially in debt to George J. Karas and to Herbert Orth, chief and deputy chief of Time-Life photo labs, and to Carmine Ercolano, supervisor of black-and-white, and Peter Christopoulos, supervisor of color, who were responsible for processing all the photographs in this book.

At Simon and Schuster we had the benefit of Alice Mayhew's enthusiasm and fine editorial pencil, and of Gwen Edelman's patient support.

Shelley Mydans and Laurie Mamo checked the manuscript with authority and imagination.

New York, N.Y.   M.D.
May 1, 1979   C.M.

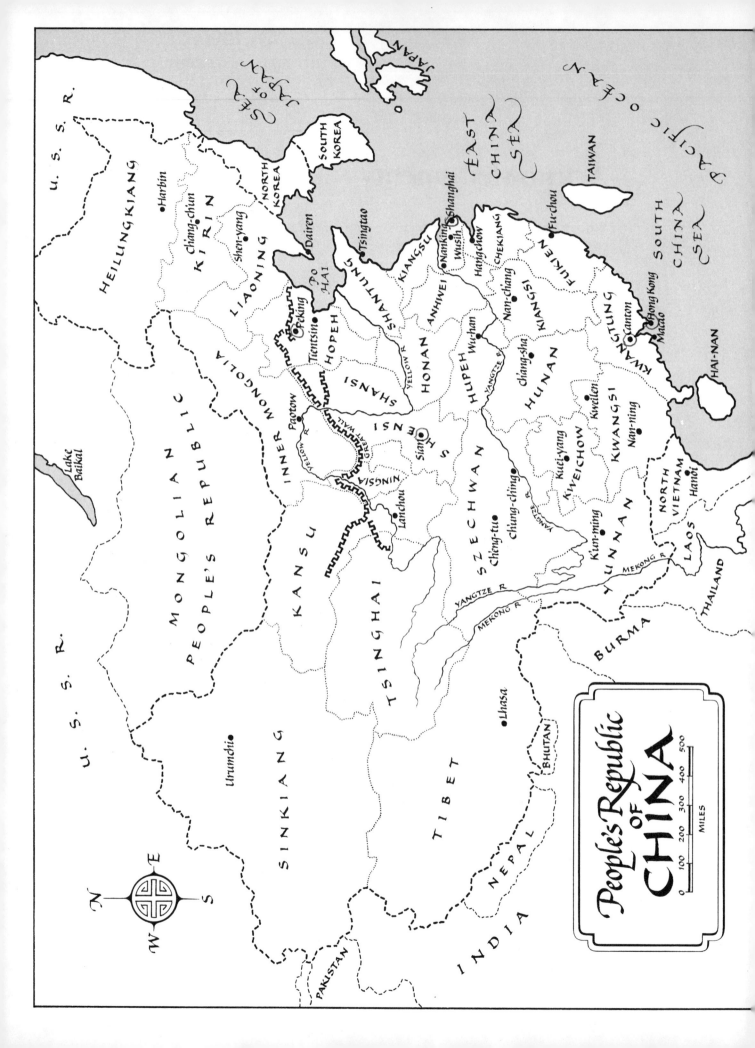

Contents

Introduction
The Colossus Sheds Its Cocoon
-and Says *Ni Hao!* - - -

It may be more important today than ever before for the
westerner to have an understanding of what is going on in
China, and what life is like in that vast country. Almost daily,
news stories from around the world report some new diplomatic
or strategic move, economic pact or domestic reform initiated by
the People's Republic. Piecemeal, they chronicle China's abrupt
determination to wrench itself headlong into modernity and
power. Overall, they reflect a nation that is united, self-confident
and outward-looking after years of isolation and sanguinary
ideological turmoil—a backward, revolutionary, traditionally
xenophobic society that is boldly, even hungrily, reaching out to
the West.

China's new leap outward will plainly affect the rest of the
world. This is so not only because it is the planet's most
populous nation with perhaps one billion inhabitants, one-fourth
of the world's population. The eventual emergence of this
basically agrarian society as an advanced industrial power will
reshape the geopolitical maps. China's new economic
partnership with its old enemy Japan; its still fragile but
blossoming friendship with a onetime ally and more recent *bête
noire*, the United States; its closer relations with Western
Europe—all these developments presage a global shift of
allegiances, interests and influence. It is no wonder that China's
current archfoe, the Soviet Union, is deeply disturbed by the
stirring in Asia.

China, for so long a cocooned colossus, seems determined
now to occupy an economic and political role consonant with its
size and vast undeveloped resources. At the same time, its new
leadership is committed to raising the living standards of its
people, a notoriously hazardous undertaking in a Communist
society. To attain their economic, scientific, military and social

goals, the Chinese are scouring the world for steel mills, textile factories, fertilizer and automobile plants, commercial and military aircraft, mining machinery, computers, construction equipment, freighters, atom smashers and space satellites. They need foreign technology and managerial expertise in fields ranging from hydroelectric dams to hotels and highways to development of offshore oil reserves that may prove to be the world's largest. ARCO NOW TEST DRILLING (10|81)

These are astounding developments from a country that has long spurned western ways. The People's Republic, while possessing nuclear weapons, still runs largely on manual labor, pushcart and water buffalo, abacus and bicycle. Moreover, for almost a decade China's educational system was virtually closed down, costing the nation perhaps one million of the graduates, notably engineers, scientists and managers, whom it now so urgently needs. No small indicator of China's decision to open westward are the 10,000 students it will send at huge expense to universities in the U.S., Canada, Australia and Europe—regardless of the risk of their exposure to capitalist seductions.

More important, as far as the interested, unofficial westerner is concerned, was the government's decision in early 1978 to stimulate the tourist trade. While Europeans and overseas Chinese had been fairly free to visit China, Americans had not. Now, not just to satisfy the curiosity of Americans, but also to win a degree of sympathy for this Marxist society, and to earn a rich cash crop of dollars to help finance the country's technological shopping spree, the government allows Americans to enter China without difficulty. They find the WARMLY WELCOMING signs that greet them to be literally true. *Ni hao!* How do you do! say the Foreign Friend's hosts, official and unofficial, on and off the beaten tourist track, with the widest, whitest smiles in the world. The only limitation is a practical one: China has insufficient tourist facilities for the huge number of would-be visitors; and such facilities as there are, however politely offered, are far below the standards of the international traveler.

If all this seems like a complete *volte-face* in Chinese policy, it is in fact more of a delayed—long-delayed—reaction. For most of its 4,000 continuous and often glorious years of civilization, the Middle Kingdom looked disdainfully on the rest of the world. Not until the closing decades of the Ch'ing dynasty (1644–1912), China's last imperial regime, did those astute, pragmatic people realize the price of splendid isolation. From the foreign powers that ran large areas of their country as virtual colonies, they learned bitterly that history and culture were not enough, that they had lagged fatally behind the outside world they had scorned. The nation known as "the land of famine" recognized that only through western-style industrialization could it hope to regain its destined "rightful place."

It was not until the 1949 revolution—the Chinese prefer to call it The Liberation—that they were able to move toward that goal under the aegis of Chairman Mao Tse-tung, then an ardent proponent of modernization. In 1966 there ensued a decade of disastrous internal disruption—the Cultural Revolution, the rule of the Gang of Four—and an era of hostility between, on the one hand, their onetime ally, the United States, and their longtime foe, Japan and, on the other, a China that sorely needed their machines, credits and expertise. Moderate leaders such as Premier Chou En-lai, however, persisted in the conviction that economic advancement was China's paramount goal, and that rapprochement with Japan and the U.S. was its prerequisite. Chou's views were shared by Hua Kuo-feng, who after Mao's death in 1976 was confirmed as party Chairman; and Teng Hsiao-p'ing, the dynamic, disarming, five-foot-tall vice premier with the panda face who has emerged as the leading evangelizer of full-throttle economic advance. (Unlike most of China's leaders, who until 1978 had never traveled abroad, Teng studied in the West in the 1920s and is regarded as a pragmatist rather than an ideologue.) Since 1971, and the opening of Ping-Pong diplomacy, Washington in turn has increasingly recognized the strategic and commercial importance of friendly relations with Peking.

This perception is reciprocated. No anti-American slogans are to be seen today in China, where only a few years ago a million screaming demonstrators could be assembled in Peking's vast T'ien An Men ("Gate of Heavenly Peace") Square to denounce U.S. "imperialism." (Ironically, the rally was to protest the American war in Vietnam, a country that is now among China's most despised enemies.) The banners in airports and railroad stations and across huge public buildings carry bland exhortations to friendship between peoples and modernization "by 2000." The cult of Mao is being quietly quenched.

Indeed, the FF, the Foreign Friend, is officially a guest of the People's Republic and is made to feel like one. There may be limited modern amenities, but in dramatic contrast with the old China, the visitor will encounter no crime of any kind. The FF will savor some of the world's most elegant food, feast his or her eyes on scenery such as dreams are made of, wander bemused through some of the most magnificent monuments and landscapes ever created by man. The memories linger for a lifetime.

The People's Republic is, of course, an authoritarian society, and in some respects an Orwellian one. For the foreigner, however, in striking contrast with Russia or Eastern Europe—let alone Vietnam, North Korea or Cambodia—it is a relatively relaxed and open state in which the visitor is free to roam, photograph almost anything that strikes his fancy, talk with people and visit their homes. One leaves with an overwhelming impression of a civilization still redolent of art and poetry, exquisite civility and a kindliness of soul.

Land of Contrast and Contradiction

*Hearing something one hundred times
is not as good as seeing it once.*
—CHINESE PROVERB

No westerner visiting China for the first time can fail to be astonished by its diversity. However much he may have heard or read beforehand, the reality of this vast, bizarre, beautiful, shabby, striving land is almost bound to be overwhelming. Its rivers, deserts and mountains are memorable, to be sure. But its habitable terrain—mostly in the river valleys—has been so enhanced, embroidered and sculpted by human hands throughout the millennia of Chinese history that the country is a virtual museum. The pagodas, palaces, fortresses, tombs and gardens, even the inner-city warrens and rural hovels, are a chronicle of both the high aspiration and the ruthless exploitation of mankind's oldest continuous civilization. The China of today, the People's Republic, is as much a land of contrast and contradiction as the country of strange enticements that greeted Marco Polo in the thirteenth century.

Ancient junks and modern freighters crowd China's bustling ports.

The Bund, Shanghai's classic waterfront facade, built by the British to last forever.

Moreover, the Chinese themselves defy compartmentalization. They are at once proud of their achievements and effusively apologetic for their shortcomings. They are amiable, humorous, self-confident and (these days, at least) punctiliously polite. They are masters of internal discipline, although this can, and does, explode in periodic savagery; advocates of Socialist austerity yet incurable hedonists; old in wisdom yet affectingly innocent of the outside world they have for so long rejected.

On the muddy Whangpoo River at Shanghai, one of the world's most active seaports, the ribbed, rust-red sails of junks mingle with tankers and tugboats; fragile sampans vie for wind and current with freighters and ferries; World War II–vintage Chinese naval vessels anchor alongside spanking new ships. Over the water, shimmering in the morning haze, looms the Bund, the classic, built-for-ever European waterfront, whose ornate old banks and imperial trading company buildings are

occupied now by government and party offices and decked with the appropriate Red insignia. In their lordly shadow, in the mean streets and congeries of ramshackle housing that predate the skyscrapers, the Shanghainese labor, lounge, gossip, play, exercise, eat, sip tea and raise families in much the same way they did before either the Industrial or the Communist Revolution. To be sure, Shanghai today is a monochrome of the licentious pre-Communist city, with its dance halls, casinos, sing-song girls and elegant courtesans, strident hawkers and peddlers, bright colors and vibrant music. But one does not see their concomitant: deformed beggars, scabrous children, corpses in the gutter each morning.

The street scene is a melange of immemorial and modern. On a sidewalk, beside panniers of drying chicken feathers, red peppers and patties of mud and coal dust, citizens listen to transistor radios and take apart tractor motors. Beside a canal a young man plays "Red River Valley" on a three-string guitar.

A rooftop shed houses two families; the Forbidden City, home of emperors.

Pharmacies dispense a cornucopia of centuries-old cure-alls: snake extract for colds, ginseng cigarettes for smoker's cough, Male Silkworm Tonic for impotence—and, without prescription, antibiotics and The Pill (which has not yet entirely replaced tadpoles as a contraceptive). The Chinese rely on herbal medicine and such arcane arts as acupuncture for treatment of most ills that flesh is heir to. Yet hospitals in Peking and Shanghai are equipped with sophisticated western devices, and Shanghai's Number Six People's Hospital is world-renowned for its success in reattaching and transplanting severed limbs. The big department stores are well stocked with sophisticated consumer goods ranging from television sets to ham radio equipment—and the sales clerk figures the bill on an abacus.

Shanghai, approximately midway between Canton and Dairen on China's 2,500-mile coastline, is the world's biggest metropolitan area (population: 10.8 million) and the nation's leading trading center and second-most-important industrial

city: half of all China's exports pass over its wharves. It is a good place for the visitor to begin his tour. Peking, 675 miles to the north—25 hours by train, 2 by plane—is a strait-laced, humdrum city, seemingly overawed by its history, its dazzling architectural relics and the brooding aura of the late Chairman Mao. On the other hand, Canton, 1,093 miles south—36 hours by train, 4.5 by air—is sassy, shabby and strident, and the most westernized of China's cities. Within hiking and swimming distance of British-ruled Hong Kong and worldly, Portuguese-administered Macao, Guangzhou (Canton) province is the homeland of most overseas Chinese; its twice-yearly trade fair lures boisterous businessmen from all over the world. As for Shanghai, built and run by foreigners for a century, it is still a freewheeling, street-smart, independent city whose round-the-clock bustle, 24-hour *(jih-ye)* eating places and shops remind the visitor of New York City.

Venturing beyond Shanghai, the tourist finds a countryside even more visibly a study in contradiction. On the huge farms, the People's Communes, that exist to feed the insatiable city, there are trucks and crude tractors and small factories; there are elaborate pumping stations to irrigate the fields and drain the floods. Yet the primary means of transportation is still the human body, male and female, young and old, bowed under a yoke supporting two heavy baskets, painfully hauling overloaded carts, or pedaling bicycles built for freight. Over the intensively cropped terraces of vegetables and grain, lines of stooped peasants endlessly plant, weed, cull and pick by hand. Much of the tilling is done by water buffalo dragging Bronze Age–type shallow plows, while between the rows women prepare for the seedlings by spreading night soil, still the principal fertilizer in use. The produce and supplies may travel by hand-poled sampan (literally, "three boards"), plying China's vast network of rivers and canals, while motorized, tourist-packed cruise boats pass peasants using trained cormorants to catch fish.

In the cities, pervasive pollution . . .

20

. . . in the country, saplings and sweet air.

Faster commerce moves north-south on the national railway system, which also offers comfortable (and punctual) passenger trains (the word for train is "fire cart" but the engines are diesels). In "soft berth" (or first-class) cars, short-haul passengers are seated at linen-spread tables, each decorated with a potted plant, and served excellent meals and teas by white-jacketed attendants—in short, afforded every Victorian convenience. Most tourists, however, travel on buses, which lack air-conditioning and up-to-date suspension but, despite the interference of hordes of bicycles, trucks, tractors and horse carts (See Chapter 5), provide door-to-door service.

The Foreign Friend, as he or she is called, thus may comfortably visit museums, temples and palaces filled with resplendent artifacts of jade, porcelain, ivory and gold. Chinese archeologists continue to excavate the relics of their 4,000-year-old civilization; the 2,200-year-old tomb of Emperor Ch'in Shih in the Yellow River Valley, for instance, recently has yielded 7,000 life-size pottery horses and warriors, with perhaps 30,000

New high-rises house some workers, but most live in cramped, primitive quarters.

more still underground. Chinese sightseers outnumber foreigners at most historic sites.

Although many ancient temples, churches and monuments are abandoned or used as warehouses, and sections of the Great Wall have been allowed to disintegrate, and the last remnants of Peking's city wall are being demolished to make way for a subway, countless other historic sites are sedulously maintained at heavy government expense. The Forbidden City, only lately opened to the Chinese themselves, is being painstakingly restored as a lustrous 720,000-square-meter people's palace and park open to travelers from all over the world.

In one of the few remaining pedicabs, two passengers ride in luxury; on an inland river, a fisherman rests while a cormorant works.

The demands of such travelers partly account for another, equally striking study in contrasts—the Chinese National Airline, or CAAC. Equipped with immaculate modern air terminals, it schedules only one-tenth as many flights daily from Peking as are flown from Syracuse, New York. At most airports crops press to within centimeters of the tarmac; at some, the runways are lined by military biplanes ready at a moment's notice to take off. CAAC flies an aging fleet of Tridents, Boeing 707s and Ilyushins, pending delivery of a fleet of Boeing 747s on order. The cigarette-puffing pilots, indistinguishable from other workers in white shirts and baggy blue pants, seem skillful; the prim stewardesses serve excellent candy, Chunghua cigarettes and soft drinks (nothing stronger). The seating on board is painfully cramped.

The best hotels, reserved for foreigners, are equally uncompromising. Although the modern rooms are spacious and equipped with private baths, the shower heads are shoulder high to giant Caucasians and there are no shower curtains. Managements generally furnish free cigarettes, candy, thermos flasks of hot water for tea, bottled beer, mineral water and soft drinks. The hotels also provide an outsize comb, a hairbrush and undersized sandals; coat hangers are in short supply. Room service in other respects typically consists of providing a folded top sheet and blanket dumped on the bottom-sheeted unsprung, unmattressed bed. Ice cubes are almost impossible to obtain. Moreover, hotel personnel have a disconcerting habit of entering guests' rooms without knocking. Toilets are apt to run nonstop or not at all. Tipping is forbidden, in hotels as anywhere else in China; nor are there any sales taxes.

Among other things the tourist can expect to forgo: shoeshines, nightclubs, speedways, racetracks, jukeboxes, good grape wine, cocktails, marinas, golf courses, tennis courts, surfing beaches, swimming pools, news, hamburgers, roller rinks, hiking trails, pubs, planetariums and Kleenex. On the other hand, there are no headwaiters, muggers, panhandlers, black marketeers, hagglers or visible prostitutes (discreet prostitution persists in such foreign-influenced cities as Shanghai and Canton). In any case, the traveler in China is usually content to turn in at 10 P.M.

He awakens to a melange of odors, stirred by the bedside fan—breeze-borne aromas of pines and deodars, birches and cedars, orchards and bamboo groves, jasmine and eucalyptus. . . . And, alas, automotive fumes and the ubiquitous clouds of soft-coal smoke pouring from factory chimneys, sometimes only a few hundred yards from a hotel window. (In Peking, which has become industrialized only in recent years, factories are sited to the south, so that the prevailing winds blow smoke away from the city.) Another kind of pollution—propaganda—is remarkable for its absence. No longer are public spaces plastered with anti-imperialist slogans. Mao badges have become collectors' items, and the little red book of his quotations mildews in the warehouse. (It is said that enough copies of the old book were printed for every man, woman and child in China.) Billboards concentrate on the universal theme of modernization by the year 2000, or, as at the Shanghai railway station, proclaim fortune-cookie bromides like "The Just Struggles of the People of All Countries Support Each Other."

But for all their egalitarian fervor, the Chinese are, and always have been, among the world's most status-conscious people. A welcoming committee is greatly confused, for example, if the male leader of a visiting western group, deferring to the women, does not emerge first from the plane, train or bus. They are even more disturbed by a list of visitors in alphabetical, not hierarchical, order. (How to assign the hotel rooms or arrange the banquet seating?)

There are supposedly no bosses in China, but a Most Responsible Person is accorded all the deference due a division manager or department head in the West. There are no insignia of rank in the People's Liberation Army (which encompasses all the armed forces), but only officers have four pockets on their tunics; lesser ranks have two. A high official can usually be spotted by the cut of his high-collared *chung-shan chuang*, the so-called Mao jacket; it will probably be gray, not blue, well tailored, even made of silk, and quite dashing. Of the fewer than 100,000 passenger automobiles in China, the only nontaxis are allotted to Most Responsible Persons or party cadres, whose backseat privacy is assured by frilly beige curtains.

After almost three decades of vilification and mistrust, the visiting American usually expects a less than effusive greeting in China. But he is indeed treated as the Foreign *Friend:* the smiles and *Ni haos!* are lavish and spontaneous. There are, have been and will be marked differences in national policies, but for these the visiting American is not held to account.

City Life: Crammed, Cramped, Noisy and Uncomfortable -but Seldom Dull

The streets of China's cities are an essential part of Chinese urban living space, a congruence of kitchen, dining room, bathroom, workshop, patio, parlor and playground. Just about every domestic activity is conducted in these streets. Most city dwellers are densely packed together in Dickensian quarters. One dim, dingy room per family is the norm, thirty square feet per capita, with a kitchen (if any) shared by several clans, no running water, only communal baths and toilets.

The enforced proximity of the Chinese may explain their decorum and civility. People living so closely together under the same circumstances must cooperate and tolerate to make life bearable. The rare flare-up on a city street is quickly pacified by the residents; the offenders may then be subjected to a course of "self-criticism" conducted by their peers. Urban society is governed by a network of familial and communal disciplines that have little to do with ideology. If someone is obviously living beyond his means, the neighbors will make him see the unwisdom of his ways.

One cannot help noting, however, that the first-floor windows in apartment buildings are barred, as in American cities. Most bicycles are padlocked when not in use. Moreover, even the Chinese admit that there has been an increase in crimes of violence. These are blamed mostly on the aftermath of the Cultural Revolution, when millions of youthful Red Guards were told, in Mao Tse-tung's words, that "to rebel is justified." Many of these young people were later sent to work on the communes; a number drifted back illegally to the cities, where they could not get jobs or ration cards or enroll in a university. Some formed youth gangs or embarked on free-lance careers of crime. The authorities, who had long denied the possibility of such aberrations in a Socialist society, now concede that they have set up reform schools for juvenile delinquents. There have been only one or two reports of crimes directed against Foreign

City streets are an essential part of Chinese living space—a congruence of kitchen, laundry room, bathroom, workshop, patio, parlor and playground.

On the Bund, in the old French concession and on Nanking Road, Shanghai today is a shabby, respectable shadow of the wicked old international city.

Friends, however. In his everyday dealings with the Chinese, the visitor is deeply impressed by their standards of honesty and fairness.

The People's Republic has sixteen cities with more than one million inhabitants. (In the early nineteenth century, the Middle Kingdom boasted of six of the world's ten biggest cities.) While statistically China is still overwhelmingly a rural society, it is in the densely populated cities that one can sense most keenly the nation's tempo and temperament.

City life begins, literally, at cockcrow: there are chickens on every block. At sunrise, tables are trundled out onto the sidewalk for breakfast, which may be cooked outdoors. Mothers brush and braid their daughters' lustrous black hair for school. Older girls peel and slice vegetables for the evening meal. Fathers, trying to be useful, cradle infants, split kindling, oil

bicycles or read the nonnews in the morning paper. Aunts scurry to the stores for supplies, which for lack of refrigeration have to be bought fresh every day. Grandmothers, who customarily run the household during the daytime, do the laundry and hang up the wash on bamboo poles or on trees. Old men, or younger men who have worked at night, settle down to *bai-fen*, the Chinese poker, or to dice or checkers. (Gambling is officially prohibited in China, but that particular regulation is honored in the breach.) Meanwhile, small restaurants do a lively trade in eat-in or takeout breakfasts, which may consist of rice porridge and green tea or delectable deep-fried *yu-t'iao*, a cousin to the cruller, which sells for two cents. Throughout the city, small shopkeepers roll up their blinds: cobblers, clothiers, bakers, basketmakers, bicycle repairers, tinsmiths, pharmacists, hardware dealers and sweetmeat vendors with great glass bowls of candy in every hue and flavor, all hygienically wrapped. All these shops are run by cooperatives or local government agencies. The average retail markup ranges from 4 to 7 percent (versus about 45 percent in the U.S.) There is no haggling over prices. The big department stores open later and are soon filled with curious crowds; more than 100,000 people a day visit Shanghai's Number One Department Store, the nation's best, which is busy seven days a week. (No charge accounts or credit cards are accepted, but traveler's checks can be cashed.)

Before the working day begins half of these people have turned out to exercise. On the sidewalks and streets, in gardens and parks, men and women, mostly middle-aged, somberly, silently enact the 108 prescribed movements of *t'ai-chi-ch'uan*, an ancient balletic-athletic ritual designed to invigorate the soul and tone the body. Other groups practice *wu-shu*, also mutely, a martial art that entails violent flailing of wooden swords and spears. Meanwhile, other, generally younger, Chinese jog, perform calisthenics, toss basketballs or improve their soccer skills.

Then, as if a great bell had rung, workers head abruptly for their jobs in office, factory, wharf and warehouse. Thereafter old women sweep the sidewalks with straw brooms while laborers clean the streets, manning tricycles propelling rotary brushes. No speck of litter remains. But as the streets grow clean, the air grows foul. Factories and utilities belch sulfurous fumes. The government sets no emission standards for motor vehicles, which trail invisible clouds of carbon monoxide. And as the sun rises higher, the smog descends.

Strollers in a Canton street

Bicycles, for freight or
human transport, are the
Great Wheel of China.

By 6:30 A.M., regardless of the sun's position—all of China
runs on Peking time—the cities are a madness of competing
wheels. There are only 15 miles of subway in the entire nation,
all of them in Peking. Workers jostle aboard the gray two-coach,
accordion-linked buses, which run frequently and charge only
two cents for any destination within the city. Freewheeling
citizens mount their sturdy bicycles, unisex machines that are
not equipped with manual gears, lights or pump but are plainly
built to last. In order to buy a bicycle, a worker must produce a
certificate from his place of employment stating that he needs
the wheels; then he must invest around $90, the equivalent of
three months' pay for the average factory hand. Still, there is no
shortage of bikes in China: there are two million in Peking
alone, and possibly twice as many in Shanghai. At rush hour
they become the Great Wheel of China, coolly defying the
anguished blasts and burps of motor vehicles. Adding mania to
the traffic are trucks, tractors, cars, pony carts and pedestrians
coming into the city with food for market.

White-uniformed traffic policemen in elevated cabins at
major intersections bark directions into microphones, and are
totally ignored. There are only a few hundred traffic lights in all

of China, and these too are ignored. But for all the sound and fury, there are remarkably few traffic accidents. One reason may be that few vehicles ever gain enough speed to inflict damage.

Despite the traffic jams and crowded sidewalks, the People's Republic is not the human anthill that detractors have portrayed. To be sure, it is a totalitarian society, and some of its aspects are dismayingly Orwellian. But work is not one of them. For all the slogans about building a greater Socialist society through hard labor, there are few Stakhanovites on the assembly lines. Workers take time to gossip, smoke and drink tea. The Ford Motor Company plant in Atlanta that was visited by Vice Premier Teng turns out 183,000 LTD cars a year, fourteen times the number of automobiles produced annually in all of China. Some factories faithfully make outmoded objects that might better be made in the primitive workshop of a rural commune.

Most of the productive machinery is admittedly old, perhaps thirty years out of date by American or Japanese standards. There is little automation. But, also by the standards of most industrialized nations, the obviously overmanned factories could produce a great deal more than they do. Indeed, while the peasant relies on "work points" awarded on the basis of productivity, factory workers have not generally received bonuses for meeting or exceeding quotas; many, until 1978, had not won raises for more than ten years, which led to pervasive but unpublicized slowdowns and strikes. On the other hand, while industrial workers put in eight-hour shifts six days a week, they have only six or seven days' vacation a year. Many thousands of couples are separated by jobs in different cities but are granted short visitation leaves. The high rate of absenteeism is unparalleled by any labor force in the West. Moreover, many managers are, above all, politicians, better versed in slogans than in blueprints.

For example, the director of a plant producing terra-cotta figurines in Foshan insists that its output is designed to celebrate "revolutionary soldiers and workers." In fact, what the employees are producing, rather desultorily, is pure *kitsch* designed for export to Hong Kong and Woolworth counters in the United States—and a profit. A factory in Soochow makes tons of china Santa Clauses, which do not wind up on Chinese trees. It is no wonder that many employees of such enterprises seem listless, apathetic—or absent.

———————————

More fortunate, and possibly better-motivated, than most industrial workers are the Ts'aos of Kweilin. Ts'ao Hung-ch'i and his wife, Ts'ao Su-ch'ing, both forty-two, and their eldest daughter, Ts'ao Su-wing, twenty-four, work in a factory making measuring equipment ranging from T squares to micrometers; a younger live-at-home daughter works at another plant. With four breadwinners in the household, the Ts'aos live quite comfortably. From a combined monthly income of about $117, they pay $2.40 monthly rent for a fairly spacious three-room apartment in a building that was built for workers by their factory in 1970. The rent includes electricity for four light bulbs. They have a radio and an electric fan but no television. They do not have a bathroom, running water or a kitchen; most of their meals are eaten at canteens in the factory or in their building, though the Ts'aos do have a brazier for cookouts on their balcony.

The Ts'aos share a toilet with several other families. They own three bicycles. They seem to be relaxed and comfortable; pretty Su-wing wears an attractive flowered blouse and well-fitted trousers and gets her hair cut by a hairdresser in the factory. The Ts'aos have a son in middle school whose tuition is paid by the state; so too are 90 percent of their medical bills, and they pay no income or property taxes and face only a minimal rate of inflation.

A white-collar worker—which in China means almost without exception a functionary of the state or some other public agency such as a cooperative—has greater and more visible responsibility than the shift worker but does not get paid much more and usually puts in longer hours. Mrs. Li Chung-ming of Peking would be described by western sociologists as upwardly mobile middle class. She is comely, vivacious, thirty-two years old and a graduate of Peking University. As an interpreter-guide for the China Travel Service, she speaks fair

English and absorbs more phrases avidly, daily, cherishing particularly the casual slang of the American tourist.

Mrs. Li's thirty-four-year-old husband, also a graduate of Peking University, teaches English at a high school. Their combined income: $68 a month. The Lis are lucky. They have a two-bedroom apartment on the third floor of a new high-rise, for which they pay $2.25 a month, utilities included. One of the couple's major outlays, $6 a month, is for the day-care center where their three-and-a-half-year-old son, Li Mong, spends six days a week while his parents are at work.

The Lis devote about one-third of their income to food. Their monthly rice ration, 31 catties each, the equivalent of about 15 kilos or 33 pounds, costs about $2. Husband and wife usually eat breakfast at state-run canteens. Mrs. Li starts the day with steamed bread and tea, for about 3 cents. For lunch she pays anywhere from 7 cents for a vegetable plate to 75 cents for a meat dish. But when she is escorting Foreign Friends, she gets three large meals for nothing, possibly including an extravagant banquet if she is escorting VIPs.

For meals prepared at home, Mrs. Li shops at one of the numerous, well-stocked markets near her apartment. She likes to stir-fry a dish of bean sprouts and chicken, which costs 30 cents a kilo. Her husband is partial to pork, which costs 95 cents a kilo. In the spirit of compromise, they often dine on 40 cents' worth of yellowfish—crisp, curly and caught that morning—cooked with bean curd and a rich brown broth. Dinner is served with green tea or warm beer. On a special occasion Mrs. Li may pick up a bottle of *Shaohsing chiu*, the potent reddish or yellow sweet wine made from rice.

After dinner such couples as the Lis and Ts'aos may go out, assuming there is a resident grandparent to sit with the children, which there often is. They may go to a communal hall to watch television, a very bland entertainment, or to a basketball or soccer game, both of which draw huge crowds. Alternatively they might go to the theater or just stroll in a public garden, park or zoo. (A New York business executive with close ties to China reports having spent thirty days in all exploring Peking's Forbidden City without having seen half of it.)

But most likely they will go to a movie. The urban Chinese are the world's most avid moviegoers; more than four billion tickets are sold each year. There are sixty cinemas in Shanghai alone, including one on the site of the old French *canidrome*, or greyhound track, which seats 12,000 patrons. What they are shown, for four-cents admission, most often is a highly propagandistic formula adventure film pitting dedicated young

Streets are swept by hand
and tricycle.

Friends and neighbors gather on a sidewalk; cobblers open for business.

proletarians against sinister counterrevolutionary villains. But recently they have been offered technically superior and livelier fare from Yugoslavia and Rumania. In 1979 a few American Westerns were shown, as well as Charlie Chaplin's *Modern Times* and *The Hunchback of Notre Dame*.

Opera, concert, theater and ballet performances are sold out days in advance; the severely restricted repertoire permitted during Gang of Four rule has been greatly expanded to include once-banned Chinese classics and occasional western works.

Bookstores and libraries are well stocked and crowded. Many writers who were purged during the Cultural Revolution have been rehabilitated, some posthumously. Shanghai bookstores sell English-language editions of some non-Marxist American and European authors. Month-old copies of *Time* and *Newsweek* (but not *Playboy*) can be perused at university libraries. Chinese immigration and customs authorities—unlike their Soviet counterparts—do not search the visitor's baggage for potentially corrupting literature. In fact, although China is by any measure a highly repressive society, its bureaucracy appears to be remarkably benign.

A more insidious threat to Chinese cultural vitality today is the enduring legacy of the Cultural Revolution, which disrupted

education for a decade and cost the nation at least one million graduates that it sorely needs—scientists, engineers, doctors, industrial managers and technocrats. Almost half a generation of the ablest students were exiled from the cities to work on farms, where they were inept, unpopular and unproductive. The few candidates accepted for higher education obtained preferment on the basis of Maoist-Marxist orthodoxy and impeccable peasant parentage. Professors charged with Confucianism, capitalist revisionism and elitism were purged.

Nevertheless, there are still only enough university openings for about 5 percent of all student candidates, and China is now sending many graduates to the United States and Europe for language and science study. University admission is strictly by competitive examination. (It may not hurt if a student's parent is a Most Responsible Person; but, then, Harvard does not turn down Kennedys.)

In any case, the Ts'aos and the Lis and the Suns and the Wangs now believe that their children, already healthy, well fed and well clothed, will have a chance to ascend in China's expanding meritocracy. The young Chinese—40 percent of the

Cake and candy shops open onto the street.

44

population are under eighteen years of age—have greater political sophistication than their parents. A Chinese official, asked if he was not worried that exposure to wicked western ways might fatally corrupt the revolutionary zeal of exchange students, replied, "We can afford to lose some."

Gambling is officially prohibited, but these players carry on.

Fast food from cramped kitchens.

A back street is quiet at midday; a bookstore is crowded.

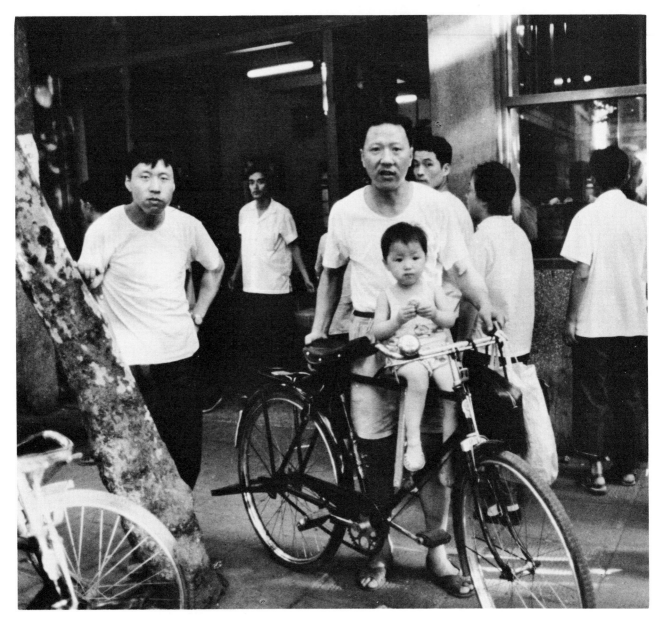

Father, son and bicycle: a familiar trilogy.

The Ts'ao family of Kweilin, five in all, pay $2.40 a month for a three-room apartment in a block of flats for factory workers.

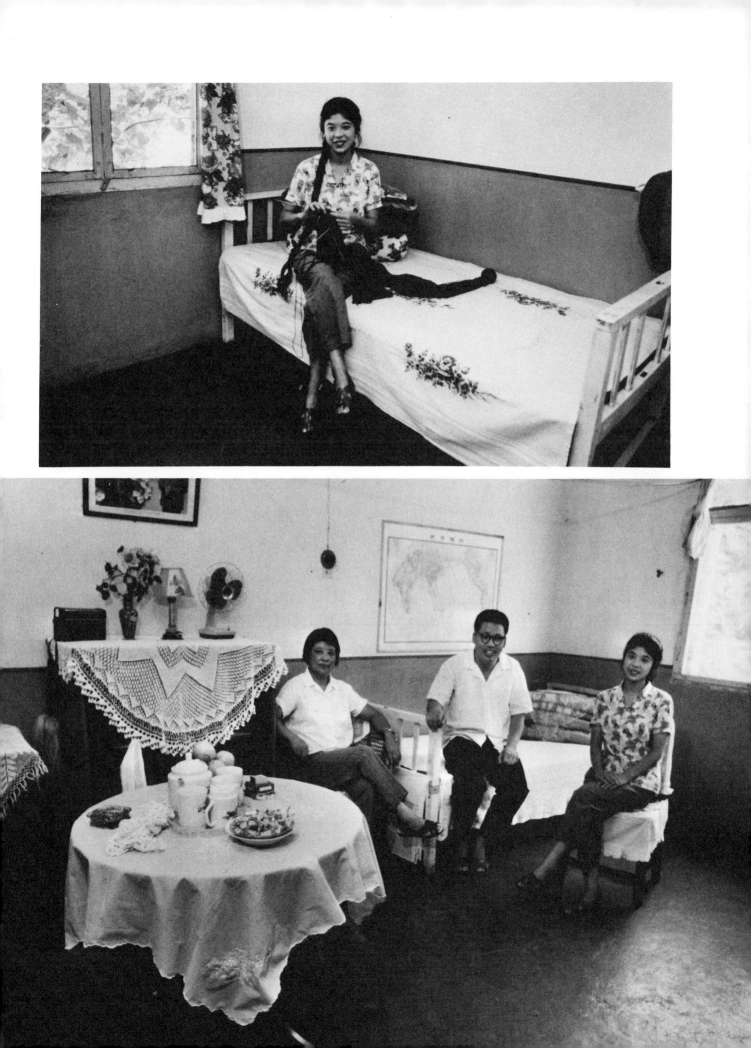

Even in the city, daily life involves carrying goods on shoulder poles, hauling water from the well.

The Busy Life of Two Wells Street

Shuang Ching, or Two Wells, Street resembles a small village in the heart of Canton. The one-block dead-end lane is insulated from the hubbub of the central city, self-contained and self-absorbed. Neighbors, who live most of their lives in close proximity, stand around and chat like countryfolk, smiling and relaxed. They show none of the tensions of inner-city life endemic to other parts of Asia. But the tempo of life in Two Wells Street is *vivace.*

Carl Mydans first observed the alley and its adjoining lanes from the veranda of his fifth-floor room in Canton's Tung Fang Hotel. For several days, at all hours, he photographed it from above with various telescopic lenses. Then he and his wife, Shelley, decided to explore it at ground level and firsthand, with an American interpreter, Tim Gelatt. They found the residents amiable and helpful; few were perturbed by the foreigners' cameras or questions. They were curious, above all. But the atmosphere was that of a composed and purposeful community of equals. No one is conspicuously rich or poor in Two Wells Street.

Soon after dawn, as the first light filters into the narrow street, doors open and chickens are let out to peck for crumbs around the houses. Then the people emerge. They start the day hauling buckets of water from the two public spigots whose sources gave the community its name. As radios carrying martial music and Chinese opera insidiously set the tempo, whole families appear and wash and brush their teeth on the street, delicately averting their eyes. This done, they chop wood, set fires in outdoor braziers, cook rice gruel for breakfast, eat it alfresco and depart for work or for the school on their block. The street teems with those who remain—mothers breast-feeding babies, fathers walking hand in hand with toddlers, older men squatting on the ground playing cards. Girls and older women go and return from nearby stores with vegetables, the rice ration and perhaps a piece of pork, chicken or fish for dinner. Presently a bicycling delivery boy passes through, distributing the local newspaper, known as a *ti-fang,* as opposed to a national paper such as *People's Daily* (which can be read on billboards downtown). This in itself is remarkable: thirty years ago the

56

Courtyards and narrow lanes lead you to dead-end Two Wells Street.

The laundry hangs out on poles in a Canton alley.

Chinese were 95 percent illiterate. The mailman also comes by each day.

Meanwhile the breadwinners, men and women, work in nearby factories, which range from light metal plants to unreconstructed sweatshops where as many as a hundred women sit shoulder-to-shoulder at sewing machines. Others have jobs right on Two Wells, which supports a number of cottage industries, or at the hotel next door. Those who remain in the street are mostly grandfathers, smoking, snoozing on cane beds, reading, doing chores, or grandmothers *(p'o-p'os)*, who look after the children, hang out the laundry, tend trays of drying peanuts and vegetables and prepare the meals. They eat three times a day, at dawn, noon and dusk, although they are given to between-meals snacks and ices on sticks. The array of food in the farmers' markets is particularly plentiful in Canton, in the so-called "land of fish and rice" south of the Yangtze. In addition to fish, mollusks, crustaceans, poultry and pork, there is an abundance of garden-fresh fruits and vegetables. One random sampling: almonds, asparagus, bananas, beans, bitter melon, cabbage, cucumber, eggplant, kale, lichees, loquats, okra, oranges, onions, pears, peas, pineapples, plums, radishes, sweet potatoes, tangerines, tomatoes, turnips and zucchini. There is also a great variety of the herbs and spices essential to Chinese cuisine, and potables of many kinds.

Most of the houses on Two Wells look very old. They are made of brick and stucco; many of the two-story buildings have a workshop below and an apartment above. The families mostly live in one or two small rooms, with a kitchen shared by two households and communal toilet facilities. Rentals and utilities cost about a dollar a month. There are no sidewalks, since there is no traffic. The street, surprisingly wide when viewed close up, is paved with granite slabs and occasional old grave markers. Two Wells boasts one four-story apartment building, which must have been built in the past decade.

The people on the street seem oblivious of the eight-story hotel for foreigners that towers above its red-tiled roofs. Obviously Two Wells at one time stretched for several blocks before it was cut off by the hotel. In deference to the sensibilities of Foreign Friends, it is said, its denizens make an effort to mute the characteristic early-morning raucousness of the inner city. Because the hotel is government-owned, and therefore visitors are deemed to be guests of the government, street dwellers seem not to resent the casual surveillance of the strange-looking, camera-clicking dignitaries.

Two Wells is modest in comparison with inner-city neighborhoods in the West, and it is a better place to live than most of the sprawling near-slums in Canton and other Chinese cities. The people have a strong sense of community. One would have to be a master criminal to steal a chicken wing. Moreover, the little cul-de-sac is neatly sandwiched between two of Canton's great adornments: Tungshan Park, overlooking the Pearl River, and Liuhua (Stream of Flowers) Park, with their lakes and boats and flowers. Within a few minutes' bike or hike is the 82-acre Canton zoo, which with some 200 species of animals and a pride of pandas is among the finest in Asia. Another park has a renowned botanical garden with more than 100 varieties of orchid. On a Sunday excursion a Two Wells family might visit the 2,400-year-old Temple of Brightness and Filial Piety; or the exquisite Flowery Pagoda in The Temple of The Six Banyan Trees, which—tradition has it—was built by an uncle of Mohammed in 626 A.D.; or White Cloud Mountain, whose peak is said to "touch the stars."

Only a few blocks from Two Wells is the Sun Yat-sen Memorial Hall, a marvelously designed theater that seats 5,000 people and offers every kind of *divertissement* from acrobatics to opera. (It is one of the few public buildings in China where smoking is prohibited.) There are movie theaters nearby, including one open-air cinema tucked under the Tung Fang Hotel. A Two Wells clan can probably afford to dine out occasionally, and the city has scores of small food shops and bistros specializing in everything from boa constrictor broth to civet cat to fragrant dogmeat stew.

One of the most remarkable restaurants in the world is the nearby Li Hua (meaning "Floating Flowers"), above a man-made 178-acre lake and park. This gastronomic emporium serves more than 10,000 meals a day. For about two dollars a family of four may have a feast—Intoxicated Shrimp, followed by Birds Eggs Stuffed with Crabmeat and Steamed in Milk, followed by Lion's Head Casserole, a concoction of pork meatballs in a gingery sauce. Freshwater fish at Li Hua come mostly from the lake outside. In the banquet rooms for Foreign Friends, the courses are served individually by waitresses and waiters, western style; in most restaurants the server sets each course in the center of the table, leaving hosts and guests to pass the plates along or winnow tidbits from a *chef d'oeuvre*. It's quite likely that Two Wells Street people have worked from time to time at Li Hua.

Two Wells Street is cut off by Tung Fang Hotel, built for foreigners, who are greeted at right by schoolchildren.

Teen-agers watch over baby brother.

The busy life of Two
Wells Street, a narrow
dead-end lane in Canton.

European-built sector of Canton.

Soochow, a city of canals.

Daybreak over the Hwangpoo River.

By dawn's early light, soul-soothing, body-strengthening exercises. Billboard in background promotes goal of modernization by 2000.

(Left) China Travel Service guide rallies his flock.
(Right) Actor flags opening of acrobatic show.

(Left) Photographing a jade Buddha. (Above) Groping through a limestone cave.

Scenes from a comic opera permitted again after being banned by the
Gang of Four.

Children performing in Shanghai.

The Peasants:
Poor, Productive and Proud

The work is grueling, the hours are long, the rewards scanty. Yet for China's 850 million peasants, life has improved beyond measure since the 1949 "Liberation." No longer at the mercy of unscrupulous landlords and tax collectors, farm workers have enough to eat and adequate if primitive medical care; their children go to school. They are fully employed and pay no direct taxes. Many own their homes. Countryfolk are abundantly proud of their accomplishments over the past thirty years. They have reason to be. The farms—the People's Communes—are the mainstay of the economy, providing the food and most raw materials needed to feed and clothe the industrial workers and 4.3 million members of the armed forces—a total population that grows by 15 million a year. . . . All this in only one-tenth of the nation's 3.7 million square miles, the small fraction that can be cultivated. China's destiny, today as always, rests on the willingness and ability of the peasants to deliver food and water to the cities.

Thus, unlike the Soviets, the Chinese authorities use more carrot than stick in dealing with the peasants. To be sure, farm workers are not permitted to migrate to the cities—unless needed—or even to move to other communes. But by largely freeing agriculture from the rigid *diktats* of the central government, Peking encourages a degree of initiative rarely found in Russia. Depending on the weather, China's annual grain production is less than 300 million tons, 500 million tons less than that of the U.S. Despite grain rationing at home, the country exports rice, vegetables and pork but has to buy wheat and soybeans abroad. Largely on their own, communes have greatly diversified their output, which may range from silkworms to mangoes, catfish to duck eggs. Moreover, they make a profit, which is shared by commune members. Much propaganda has been made of the rural workers' heroic feats in leveling mountains, reclaiming arid land and building roads, bridges, dams, hydroelectric plants and irrigation systems. The fruits of their labor are all there to be seen.

Autumn on a commune: time to weed the second crop of short-stalk rice.

Water buffalo, beast of
all work and peasant's
best friend.

In the twenty years since it was organized, Ta Li People's Commune (population: 68,000), in the Foshan area near Canton, has leveled eleven hilltops, terraced the sides, planted 28,000 orange and mandarin trees on them and doubled the rice crop; the communards also have built a striking Romanesque aqueduct to water their fields. The Hsinching Commune (population: 21,626), an hour's drive from Shanghai, has built eleven pumping stations to irrigate the crops and drain flood waters, meanwhile raising its production of vegetables alone by 300 percent since 1949; its shipments of vegetables to the city—122 varieties, they claim—are sufficient to feed 300,000 people for a year. One commune boasts of meeting some of its energy demands with methane gas made by its own process from sewage and garbage. At another, in Hunan, the peasants have built a mill to make paper out of rice stalks, using power from a hydroelectric dam they had completed earlier. Moreover, these undertakings are almost entirely conceived and executed without technical or financial help from the government. Almost half of China's farmland is now irrigated.

Freight is hauled by backpower or bicycle; roads are built with pick and shovel.

70

Schoolgirls and mothers in a market town.

While some production claims seem inflated, and may be partly explained by the absorption of neighboring acreage, there is no doubting the industriousness and inventiveness of the farmers. It is equally obvious that the most successful communes have capable leaders, who are elected, not imposed from above (unlike the bureaucrats of regional and national regimes).

Just about every commune combines food production with small-scale industry. This assures full use of man (and woman and child) power, since, even though most farms raise two or three crops a year, there are slack seasons in the fields. The Hsinching Commune, for example, has a primitive machine shop that not only keeps its own farm equipment in repair but also subcontracts parts for a bigger factory. Ta Li makes its own electric pumps, bricks, cement and furniture. Other rural enterprises include cotton gins, oil presses and small tractor plants or engage in boat building, pottery making, basket

weaving and jade carving. At some communes women and children use their spare time to make firecrackers, of which the Chinese must be the world's most exuberant users.

In all, there are some 50,000 communes, most of which have more than 10,000 inhabitants. (There are no private farms in the People's Republic.) The work is divided among "production brigades" organized in teams of from 15 to 30 households each. Individual members are paid in "work points," awarded on the basis of performance in field or factory and decided after twice-annual personal evaluations worthy of the flintiest capitalist corporation. The commune's income is roughly what is left after production costs, taxes, capital improvements and mandatory sales of grain to the state (about 5 percent of the total).

According to a folk saying, "Women hold up half the sky." Yet, despite immense gains in women's rights, male farm laborers are still paid more than female, even though the latter may work as hard or harder; moreover, women get no work points for looking after home and family. Each family has on average a half-acre on which it can raise vegetables, poultry and

A farm girl ladling nightsoil over rows of cabbage.

Work brigade of Ta Li People's Commune terraced eleven hills, built
an aqueduct for irrigation and planted orange groves.

pigs for its own consumption or for extra cash. Twice a year each receives an allotment of grain and cooking oil, the cost of which is deducted from work-point income. Other supplies are bought from a communal distribution center that, apart from such exotica as dried fish, Three Snake Wine and pickled lotus root, resembles an American country store.

One couple among the hundreds of millions who keep the Chinese agricultural system working are Ch'en Ho-kuang, thirty-nine, and his wife, Ch'en Yen-liu, thirty-six. They live with three young daughters in Hao Mei village, part of the Ta Li Commune mentioned previously. Like their neighbors, they own their whitewashed brick house, in a row of ten attached dwellings on a narrow lane. The house, which is fairly new, has a tile roof and a tile floor. Its sixty square meters of floor space embrace a small entry hall, a large living room, a moderate-sized bedroom and a small brick kitchen, where the rice is stored in big earthenware crocks. The family has its own privy in a small courtyard; bathing is done in a communal facility.

The Ch'ens' house is not uncomfortable, although it gets hot in summer and cold in winter, and it is well furnished: three beds, a desk, a small glass-covered dresser, a big table, eight or ten chairs. Decorations include the typical portraits of chairmen

Lighted map of Ta Li Commune, where transport ranges from tractor to hand-hauled cart.

Mao and Hua, several large prints of fruit and flowers, and a
swatch of bright wallpaper. The bedroom entrance is curtained
with printed cloth. The Ch'ens have five of the prized "things
that go round": an electric clock, a three-speed fan, a sewing
machine and two bicycles, as well as a fluorescent light tube.
They have a radio but no television. The house cost about $600
to build on free land.

Before leaving for the fields in the morning, Mrs. Ch'en
slices the vegetables for lunch and leaves them covered in a wok
on the brick stove. She returns at midday to prepare the meal for
herself and her daughters, who come home from the nearby
school. The mother stir-fries an aromatic blend of beans and taro
root, while the eldest daughter, eleven-year-old Ch'en Yen-heng,
feeds rice stalks into the crackling stove. Many farms at one

At Hao Mei village, fishponds add to the food supply, firecracker manufacture to the commune's income.

Whole families turn out to make firecrackers in their spare time.

point set up communal dining halls to save women like Mrs. Ch'en the productive time lost in cooking, but most of these mess halls have been eliminated. A member of the "revolutionary committee" (i.e., board of directors) at one commune explains: "The people all ate too much."

The Ch'ens have a net income of around $30 a month, not counting earnings from their private plot. Small as that seems, they pay no rent or taxes, spend little for food or utilities and almost nothing for medical care or education, and have a small savings account that returns 2.5 percent. Moreover, they will earn more when their children are old enough to make work points in the fields. Their neighbors, the Wus, have more than twice as much take-home pay because there are five working members of the family. They have a slightly larger house with an upstairs room, and Mrs. Wu allows herself the luxury of several kittens in the home. (There are few cats in China and even fewer dogs, the reason being that they are perceived to dirty the streets and consume valuable food.)

While peasants the world over rejoice in large families, if only as a form of social security, the Chinese at the commune

and city-block level have responded to one of the world's most extensive and effective birth control programs; the Wus almost certainly would not have had seven children if they had married only ten years ago. The birth rate is estimated at 2.5 percent, while the infant mortality rate is about that of most industrialized societies. Average life expectancy has lengthened dramatically, from 28 years in 1947 to 65 today. Thus, population growth is a constant challenge to agriculture.

Dangling the carrot, the government has promised that all peasant children will be able to finish high school by the early 1980s, but it is hard to imagine that many of those who go on to university will return willingly to a life of stoop labor. On the other hand, the Chinese countryman seems deeply attached to his beautiful land, the forests and peaks, rivers and lakes; above all perhaps to the sense of fulfillment that every good farmer feels when the crops are tall and the chickens fat.

Furthermore, life on the communes may become easier. Rural officials repeatedly, apologetically refer to the "backwardness" of Chinese agriculture. It is woefully short of fertilizer and farm machinery; every commune needs more

trucks, modern tractors, combine harvesters, threshers, milling machines, even bicycles. The farms badly need an American-style rural electrification program. Most of all, for more efficient production and distribution, the countryside needs modern roads, which would entail a vast public expenditure. Much of rural China's produce has to be shipped to market on human backs, bicycles or hand-poled sampans. (Even so, in the summertime at least, it seems to arrive in better condition than much of the produce displayed in American supermarkets.)

The Ch'en family in Hao Mei have a courtyard privy, cook on a brick stove.

The government has repeatedly pledged that agriculture will be 70 percent mechanized by 1980. This is a formidable task and, paradoxically, it may be complicated by the ambitiousness of the communes themselves. Already in some areas canny managements have switched acreage from basic foodstuff production to more lucrative crops such as tobacco. Also, with a profitable minifactory in its midst, a commune may well be tempted to pull workers in from the field to man the lathes. If the rural factory is selling parts to another, bigger enterprise, and the plant up the line decides to increase production, the commune may have to scavenge for scarce steel or other materials on the expanding gray market. This process nowhere matches the monumental distortions prevalent in the Soviet economy, but it is a threat to the present flexibility and efficiency of the food-producing sector.

The rural populace, then, fares decently. Moreover, the nation's grandiose goals of modernization may be helped because the majority of its people are still proud to be peasants.

One Way or Another, They (and the Visitor) Get Around

Just about every form of transportation ever invented is to be seen in China. People and goods travel by truck, tractor, bus, taxi, official limousine, boat, airplane, bicycle, tricycle, pedicab ("three-wheel-cart") propelled by pedal or motor, cart, wagon, wheelbarrow, horse, water buffalo, and by camel in Sinkiang and yak in Tibet. (The man-killing ricksha was mercifully abolished by the People's Republic after 1949, although a few still are used in the Crown Colony of Hong Kong.) Men and women balance heavy baskets on shoulder poles and push incongruous loads on handcarts. One of the more ingenious forms of transport involves a linkage of two bicycles, which enables workers to

China has 100,000 miles of waterways, including the Li River at Kweilin.

Freight and passengers
move by tractor, train
and junk . . .

. . . by strings of barges, workboats on a commune canal and the ubiquitous bike.

94

haul, say, a load of eighteen-foot timbers. There are surprisingly few motorcycles, and no motorscooters or mopeds. Traffic in China officially moves on the right-hand side of the highway, but most motor vehicles hog the middle of the road.

China's highway system is still rudimentary. Most of its 500,000 miles of road are dangerously narrow, unpaved and impassable in bad weather. Improvement and extension of road transport is an important part of the modernization program. On the other hand, vast amounts of freight and human cargo travel over China's 100,000 miles of navigable waterways and along its 2,500-mile coast. The craft range from junks and sampans, some motorized but mostly under sail or hand-poled, to big, modern ferryboats that provide the country's most economical long-distance passenger transportation: third-class from Dairen to Shanghai, for example, for about $7, considerably less than the rail fare. Big seagoing ships can go as far up the Yangtze as Wuhan, 600 miles inland from Shanghai. Many of the sampans on the rivers and canals belong to people's communes, which depend on them to get their goods to market and ship back materials like fertilizer and bricks. While boat people used to live their entire existence on fishing or freight-carrying sampans, the Chinese claim that they virtually all now have housing ashore. China's international ports are hopelessly congested; ships often wait weeks for dock space.

A ferry is steered by oar; peasants pole a skiff.

Sampans fishing in the
East China Sea.

Public transportation in the cities is crowded but efficient and cheap. The articulated electric trolleybuses and diesel buses run frequently and charge about two cents to any destination. Shanghai alone has 152 bus lines. Peking's subway, which at present runs only fifteen miles into the western suburbs, is being extended northward. Visitors find the system effective, reasonably comfortable and inexpensive: five cents a trip. In the event of war, the subways, like the London underground during the blitz, would be a vast air raid shelter.

Few Foreign Friends, however, use public transportation in the cities, if only because of the language barrier. Much of their traveling is done on tourist buses, which allow little legroom and on long trips also can be hard on the posterior. The China Travel Service has begun importing Japanese buses that are well sprung, air-conditioned and heated—but still cramped by western standards. Taxis are inexpensive, honestly run and available. A foreign tourist's interpreter or hotel clerk will instruct, or write out directions for, the driver.

As noted earlier, CAAC, the national airline, is expanding its internal fleet of aircraft and limited facilities. When it accepts delivery of its Boeing 747s on order, passengers may even be able to get an inflight banquet. (Some airports, notably Peking's, do have pleasant restaurants.) China for some time has been exploring the possibility of regular service to and from the United States and Europe.

The railroads offer the most rewarding and comfortable way to see China—as indeed they do in any country that is sensible enough to preserve good train service. Since 1949 the nation has almost doubled its rail trackage, to more than 30,000 miles; the ailing American railway grid is about nine times as big. First-class accommodations—which cost about half as much as airline travel—consist of a European-style compartment with four beds. (As most visitors come in organized groups, one does not usually have to sleep across from total strangers.) It has a table, washbasin, and bunks at right angles to the tracks; as in Chinese hotels, the accommodations include flowers, lidded cups with packages of tea and a thermos of near-boiling water. There is also a device to turn off the loudspeaker that starts at six with martial music. Western toilets are available on some long hauls, although simpler facilities are still usual. The cars are kept scrupulously clean and are well attended, the trains move swiftly and the dining cars serve excellent five-course meals.

Tourist Treasures for Eye, Mind, Palate and Remembrance

You cannot see the flowers while riding on horseback.
—CHINESE PROVERB

Seeing China close up is as much an education as a vacation. But it is not for the infirm or lazy. The foreign tourist is engulfed in a whirl of organized activity that spins him from breakfast (or earlier) to bedtime. The sights and sensations may blur the mind and blister the feet, but the cumulative effect is overwhelming.

Whether the visitor arrives by air or ship, or by train from Hong Kong, he will encounter a minimum of immigration and customs red tape. Because group travel is a necessity—there are simply not enough bilingual guides to escort loners—cordial, efficient China Travel Service (Luxingshe) staffers will be waiting. Transportation, hotel rooms, meals and sight-seeing are admirably organized, and while the tourist's time is tightly programmed, the schedule usually allows several hours a day for shopping, rest and individual exploration.

Because of the shortage of facilities and personnel, only about thirty cities were open to foreigners by mid-1979. However, the government has indicated that in 1980 and 1981 the list will be lengthened considerably to include, among other areas, Szechwan, Sinkiang, and possibly Tibet.

In 1978, 100,000 foreigners visited the People's Republic. This number was expected to double in 1979, and just about every tour was sold out at least a year in advance. For Americans, the rush to China represents a dramatic change from 1977, when only a few favored individuals, such as doctors, scientists, scholars and businessmen, were allowed to enter the country. The Great Leap Outward and resumption of diplomatic relations with America have changed this. The Chinese today are urgently in need of foreign technology, and thus of foreign exchange and foreign support. They would surely roll up the Bamboo Curtain altogether if they had the first-class hotels, transportation and interpreters to handle the influx.

As it is, the government has contracted with a number of foreign companies to build hotels and motels in more than thirty cities, notably Peking, Shanghai, Canton, Hangchow, Kweilin,

China Travel Service guides escorting passengers from the *Lindblad Explorer.*

103

At Soochow's Tiger Hill, tourists photograph the leaning pagoda and
walk through a moon gate in the garden.

Harbin, Dairen, Nanking, Sian (the ancient capital) and perhaps Lhasa, the Tibetan capital. The new hotels, to be designed and initially managed by westerners, will come equipped with such luxuries as swimming pools, saunas, bars, coffee shops, air-conditioning and central heating.

The government is enlarging airport landing strips to handle jumbo jets, expanding the small, overage national airline, and planning Japanese-style superexpress trains. It is training brigades of interpreters. The country's diligent travel promoters hope to add such lures as big-game hunting, skiing, freshwater and deep-sea fishing, mountaineering and camel safaris.

The prospect of such development is daunting. For even in present circumstances the days are not long enough to do justice to the Forbidden City (now styled the Former Imperial Palaces), a 250-acre congeries of pavilions and pleasure domes housing the vast royal collections of gold, silver, porcelain, ivory and jade art assembled over 500 years. The Temple of Heaven, which actually consists of many temples in a 16-square-mile park, is dominated by one of the most exquisite buildings in China, the Hall of Prayer for Good Harvests. Similarly, northwest of the capital, the Summer Palace, rebuilt in 1888 by the deranged Empress Dowager Tz'u-hsi with funds misappropriated from the navy, takes days to fully appraise. About 30 miles north of Peking are the Ming Tombs, whose first occupant, the Emperor Yung-ho, the founder of Peking, was buried sixty-eight years before Columbus sighted America.

A few hours further north is the Great Wall, a 2,800-mile rampart built of granite and brick to repel Mongol barbarians from the north; it was not breached until 1449, some 2,300 years after it was begun. Few western tourists can hope to see everything—the Marco Polo Bridge; the Temple of the Reclining Buddha; Coal Hill, where the last Ming emperor hanged himself from a locust tree in 1644; the celebrated Peking zoo (formerly known as the Zoo of Millions of Animals); Peking University, on a former imperial estate; the Peking library, with its eight million books; the once-glorious Peking opera, only now recovering from the rigid strictures of the Cultural Revolution; the Museum of Chinese Art; the Museum of Natural History; and verdant Sun Yat-sen Park.

Moreover, there is much more to see than the monuments. Apart from the tombs, temples and museums—the palaces and pagodas of the Middle Kingdom—there is the living China, a nation that cannot fail to intrigue. In commune, factory, park or city street, the Foreign Friend is received with a warmth that is often overpowering.

For his part, the Caucasian is still a rarity in Chinese eyes. He/she is probably very tall by Chinese standards and physically idiosyncratic, even in relation to other Caucasians. The Han people, who constitute 94 percent of the Chinese population, on the other hand, are quite homogeneous in appearance: slight, small-boned, small-nosed, dark-eyed, black-haired, fresh-complexioned; and the women are small-breasted.

Although extremely reserved in their dealings with foreigners in the past, most Chinese today are surprisingly forthright in discussing their country, its problems present and past and their own hopes and circumstances. On the other hand, they are curious about life in the West and ask all manner of personal questions without embarrassment. The new openness, in marked contrast to the fearful reticence of Soviet citizens, occasionally extends to inviting a Foreign Friend home. At one commune, festooned with hand-lettered boards of welcome, the Most Responsible Person was observed telling a group of Americans with every evidence of sincerity: "Your visit is an inspiration to us!" In the back streets of Wusih, a quintet of *meikuo jen* (Americans) caused a traffic jam as scores of rush-hour bicyclists dismounted to chatter, grin and cry *Ni Hao!*

"The best diplomacy," according to a Chinese proverb, "is through the stomach," and the Chinese are good wok diplomats. At its best, their culinary art is among the most varied and inventive on earth. There are at least 7,000 *basic* dishes in the repertoire and more than a dozen regional cuisines, with many urban variants. Between Peking and Canton, there is far greater diversity than between, say, New Orleans and San Francisco or Provence and Paris.

The most renowned menus are Cantonese, the food of the South; Pekinese, the northern cuisine; the peppery dishes of Szechwan and Hunan; and Shanghainese cooking, which is heavier and spicier than the Cantonese. One can find restaurants specializing in such wild-game delicacies as tiger and bear paws; turtle dishes; *dim sum*, the brunch or teatime dumplings; snakes skinned live and broiled at the table; a whole menu based on dog meat; a Nanking *spécialité*, Mongolian barbecued beef; Muslim scorched beef; or mutton fire pot with bean-flour noodles and spicy minced watercress. The visitor may spend weeks in China without having the same dish twice.

Many specialties sound more exotic than they really are. The cuisine is basically one for survival, in which every usable

Shopping for postcards
and (below) embroidered
sleeve bands.

108

Just about every Foreign Friend will
visit a Friendship Store, attend
briefing sessions at commune or
factory and greet a giant panda.

sliver goes into the pot. Ducks' tongues are jellied or smoked, their feet boned and steamed; chicken entrails are pickled or finely sliced and braised; fish lips are served in brown sauce. The Chinese make edible silk purses out of sows' ears. The Manchu emperors feasted on wine-braised camel's hump; their Socialist descendants on water buffalo tail stewed in black soy sauce and anise.

George Lang, an erudite Hungarian-born restaurateur, author and designer of elegant restaurants around the world, notes that Chinese cuisine is ideally "a perfectly infused blend of ingredients, while the texture is the opposite, an entertaining conceit of using five different textures against one another." The three major elements are: *hsien*, the natural sweet flavor of fresh ingredients; *hsiang*, their enhancement by good cooking; and *hung*, the further refinement of spices and sauces. However, the ingredients and accompaniments and even the philosophies vary greatly from region to region. In the north, beef and lamb are plentiful, and breads, dumplings and noodles are preferred to rice. The central Chinese south of the Yellow River, lacking pasturage, base their recipes on pork, poultry, fish, rice and their abundant vegetables.

In Peking, *ça va sans dire*, the dish of a lifetime is Peking Duck. There is nothing like it anywhere else in the world. At Ch'uan Chu Teh (meaning "All Assembled Virtues"), almost all of the 25-course menu is virtuously assembled around duck, climaxed by the Great Dish. From the lacquered bird, thin slices of meat are enfolded in crackling caramel skin with scallions and sweet *hoisin* sauce and lovingly encased in a thin crepe, all delicately handled by one's host.

At a formal banquet in Shanghai's venerable Peace Hotel, at which every table is decorated with a different melon sculpture and chrysanthemums and butterflies carved from carrots and turnips, a gustatory highlight is a spicy melange of vegetables, scallions and peanuts that could convert any beefeater to vegetarianism.

The masterpiece of the meal at the Soochow Hotel is Beggar's Chicken, so called—legend has it—because a poor man stealing a chicken once wrapped it in mud to disguise his loot. The bird named for him is stuffed with mushrooms, bamboo shoots, pigeon eggs, shrimp and chopped pork, wrapped in lotus leaves, plastered with clay and baked for four hours. A most important guest is sometimes allowed to crack the potterized poultry with a golden hammer. Another subtle grace note: bitter-melon-based bouillon with little yellow-eyed ducks made of egg white floating on the surface.

110

Kweilin's Li River Hotel concocts a crisp, sweet-and-sour mandarin fish, stuffed with ham, sausage, onion, potato, mushroom and ginger, and sculpted to resemble a flying squirrel.

In Canton, where delicacy of taste and texture is equated with perfection, master chefs such as sixty-six-year-old Mr. Chou at the Tung Fang steam or stir-fry most dishes, which are lightly sauced so as not to hide the freshness of the ingredients. The shrimp, they say in Canton, come wriggling to the table. Pan Hsi, overlooking a man-made lake owned by the parks department (which has exclusive fishing rights), is a vast complex of dining rooms, with an airy upstairs pavilion reserved for special occasions. The restaurant employs 40 cooks, 60 kitchen helpers and 200 waiters and waitresses. Its masterpiece: Phoenix Meets Dragon in Brilliant Courtyard, a simmering wedding of chicken breasts (symbol of femininity) and ham (for masculinity). While the Chinese do not greatly prize desserts, Pan Hsi's red bean sundae is excellent.

———————

A banquet usually consists of several dozen well-orchestrated delicacies escalating in importance as the meal progresses. (Tourists are well advised not to gorge themselves on the overtures so that they have no spirit left for the arias.) Banquet protocol prescribes one big glass and two shot glasses beside each place setting. The big glass is for beer, soda or a soft drink, which is served at once and may be consumed at will. The small ones are reserved for *mao-tai*, a colorless 160-proof liquor made from sorghum known to old China hands as "rocket juice," and the *Shaohsing chiu* rice wine. Both potions are strictly for toasts; the guest waits to raise either glass until his hosts invoke the appropriate cue, such as "Friendship Between Our Peoples." Toasts are accompanied by cries of *Kan-pei!* Bottoms up! (literally, "Dry glass!"), after which toasters and toastees hold their glasses upside down. Several hosts suggest that one should not try to *sip* the libations: "That way you get headache!" One feels that anything less than *kan-pei* is only half a blow for friendship. Amazingly, multiple *mao-tais* do not seem to induce hangovers.

There are almost as many varieties of Chinese wine as there are inflections in the Chinese vocabulary. One of the strongest, *wu-chia-p'i*, is often drunk with soda as a highball. Others—*kao-liang*, made of sorghum; *mei-kwei-lu*, called Rose Dew wine; Three Snake Wine, so-called because a serpent is coiled at the bottom of the bottle—are drunk neat. All are made from rice or sorghum and are mostly sweet. There are red and white grape wines, but of no distinction, mainly for foreigners, for whose benefit the Chinese also make brandy and champagne, whiskey, gin, vermouth and an agreeable vodka (*fu-te-ka*), which is exported to the United States under the Great Wall label. The People's Republic will soon be importing, along with Coca-Cola, scotch, American bourbon and rye, and Canadian whiskey. One beverage the Chinese do not have to import is tea, of which there are infinite varieties. A few are superb; many are inferior.

To return briefly to culinary protocol, as a matter of politeness the Foreign Friend should always use chopsticks at lunch and dinnertime. These implements are, after all, designed to grasp the diced or shredded morsels that are the mainstay of Chinese cookery. Knives, forks and spoons, on the other hand, are the accepted implements for a western-style breakfast, which most foreigners prefer. Some hotels serve the standard ham and eggs with toast and marmalade; others produce such variants as fish-flavored omelette, jasmine teacakes and jelly roll. The coffee can be surprisingly good. However, the alternative menu (back to chopsticks) can be a minibanquet, such as one served at the Tung Fang Hotel in Canton: *congee* (hot rice porridge) with flakes of fish and scallions, meat filled *dim sum* (dumplings), roast pork, fried salt-water dough stuffed with dried shrimp and vegetables, the cruller-like *yu-t'iao*, sesame buns filled with soy paste, coconut cake and egg custard flan. All in one meal—but no *mao-tais*.

The acquisitive tourist intent on devouring China may further appease his appetite by buying Chinese artifacts to take home. Despite the theoretical abolition of the merchant class, department stores, Friendship Stores and back-street shops proffer a great variety of goods from *kitsch* to fine-looking wares.

The department stores—Peking's Pai Huo Ta Lou ("High Building With 100 Goods"), Shanghai's Number One, Wusih's The East Is Red—are worth visiting if only for sociological interest. They are amply stocked with well-made goods, ranging from basketball shoes to toy machine guns, textiles to TV sets. The merchandise is mostly for domestic consumption, but the visitor may want a gaily decorated thermos ($1) for cool tea during the bus ride, or an alarm clock with a panda face for rising, or a sturdy Mao jacket ($11) and matching cap ($1.50) to jolt the folks back home.

Friendship Stores are reserved for foreigners. While they vary greatly in quality from city to city, most of them offer a seductive array of rare and lustrous objects: porcelain, embroidery, silks, furs (sable, otter, mink), scroll paintings, calligraphy, lacquerware, ivory carvings, jewelry of ivory, silver, quartz and jade (which Confucius called the "virtuous gem"), snuff and perfume bottles, many-hued bargain-priced cashmere sweaters, silken fans and parasols and occasionally some elegant antique furniture. The Shanghai Friendship Store has a wistful counter full of bric-a-brac "liberated" from British offices and houses after the Revolution—to wit, Asprey's cigarette cases, soda siphons, Wedgwood dishes, fob watches, cigar cutters and tortoiseshell picture frames, all with the imprint of Bond Street.

But it is in the back streets, in small, open-front shops that have changed little over the centuries (though they are now owned by cooperatives or state agencies), that the visitor can sense China *sans* ideology, a comfort-loving, comfort-providing society that still has the skills and the time to produce artifacts of beauty and no social relevance whatever. In such stores, which cannot earn much foreign currency, as they are off the beaten tourist track, one can find a multiplicity of small marvels: silk shirts, furs, leather for wear or decoration, hand-painted nesting boxes in all shapes and sizes, lacquered woven bamboo handbags, cloisonné bangles, ceramic *poudriers* that can be used as cigarette boxes, carvings of all kinds, table linens and beautiful bamboo furniture that unfortunately would cost twenty times the purchase price to ship home. Some of the portable objects sell in expensive American stores for ten times the going price on a back street in China.

———————

The tourist itinerary includes visits to arts and crafts centers where ancient skills have been preserved and revived—and the products there too are for sale. The Shanghai Arts & Crafts Research Institute, housed in a stately mansion in the old French concession, employs 120 workers at a dozen different specialties, notably needlepoint, wood carving, silk embroidery and porcelain painting. At Soochow's Embroidery Research Institute (just about every working plant is called a research institute), artisans painstakingly thread a thousand colors of silk in traditional and modern designs, many of great beauty, some embarrassingly banal. Bigger-than-life embroideries of Mao have been discontinued for the simple reason, one official confessed, that they do not sell. An embroidered screen of goldfish, say, will fetch as much as $8,000, enough to meet the institute's payroll for a month. A dazzling four-panel embroidered screen recently was priced at $18,000 and would be worth at least twice as much in the United States. In the old days, before the 1949 Revolution, long days of minute stitching cost many workers their eyesight. Today the embroiderers, mostly young women, take periodic breaks for ocular exercises. Surprisingly, very few wear glasses.

There is no arguing over prices at any Chinese store. The attendants are scrupulously honest and patient with foreigners who are confused by the currency. A few curio shops for foreigners are managed by the same people who owned them before the Revolution.

Visitors, especially on shopping sprees away from the set itinerary, may face considerable trouble deciphering names of places and persons. The problem is a two-syllable bomb called *Pinyin*. The word, a combination of "pin," meaning phonetic, and "yin," or sound, describes a system of transliterating Chinese words into English and other languages using the Roman alphabet so that they will more closely approximate the way they actually sound. This system was officially adopted for foreign publications early in 1979, supplanting the century-old system of anglicizing Chinese ideograms. Thus the late Chairman's name is now officially Mao Zedong. Vice Premier Teng Hsiao-p'ing has become Deng Xiaoping (he admitted to American reporters that even he had difficulty adjusting to his new name). Canton, which since the Revolution has been renamed Kwangchow, undergoes another transformation: it is now Guangzhou, pronounced approximately Gwong-joe. Peking should now be called Beijing. Western cartographers estimate that there are perhaps a million place names on the map of China, and the government is only very slowly releasing the new designations. Fortunately, the visitor entering from Xianggang, a.k.a. Hong Kong, will find he is in a country that is still called China. The government in its wisdom has decreed that the mainland will not have to be called by its Pinyinized name of Zhongguo.

Chinese place names, by whatever spelling, are a particular enchantment in translation. A mountain peak overlooking the Li River is called Elephant Trunk Hill because with only a slight effort of the imagination one can make it resemble a heffalump hosing water upstream. In the hills northeast of Peking a slope on Fragrant Mountain is known as Sight That Discourages Devils. High atop multicolored Piled Silk Hill in Kweilin there is a structure called Cloud-Catching Pavilion. A 470-year-old gem in Wusih is Leave Your Pleasure Garden; tradition has it that the man who built the garden was assigned to the defense ministry in distant Peking and turned over his pride and joy to the grateful citizenry. Near The Temple of Six Banyan Trees in Canton (or Kwangchow, or Guangzhou) is The Temple of Brightness and Filial Piety. Black Tiger Spring in Tsinan is so called because of the jungle roar of water pouring from the rocks. Hangchow's Island of Lonely Hill, approached by a bridge called Western Trickling, is dominated by The Pavilion of the Autumn Moon on The Calm Lake. A 450-year-old park in Soochow bears the sardonic name of Humble Administrator's Garden, also known as The Garden of Stupid Politics, after a corrupt official who built the *plaisanterie* from stolen tax receipts. (It was later gambled away in one night by his dissolute son.) In one of Soochow's many gardens there is The Pavilion of Distant Perfumes, named perhaps for the springtime peonies, or wistfully in winter in the hope that they will soon be back.

Far from familiar panaceas, the Foreign Friend should come provided with antihistamine cold pills, an antidiarrhetic, cough medicine (though in some cities there is an effective palliative called Cough Juice), an antibiotic in case of lower respiratory infection from smog and dust, and perhaps facial tissues and a first-aid kit. Chinese hotels have good soap and better toilet paper than some of the best hotels in Europe. Smokers should bring western pipe tobacco and cigarettes. In winter the visitor should pack long johns or thermal underwear, gloves and a warm hat; heating in a Chinese bus or hotel room is uncertain at best. In summer the male visitor needs only a few short-sleeved wash-and-dry shirts and a few pairs of slacks; women should bring equally washable attire. One does not wear jackets, neckties, miniskirts or see-throughs in China. Solid crepe-soled walking shoes are a must for the endless trudge.

The visitor should also bring plenty of film; the Chinese product is inferior (though if a camera malfunctions the Chinese can repair it—or almost anything else—in minutes). As noted earlier, the Chinese do not accept tips; they regard them as insulting. However, with interpreter-guides, Responsible Persons

Inspecting calligraphy by Chairman Mao; trying on Mao jacket.

and others whom one grows to like and appreciate, it is possible to convey some small token of gratitude and, yes, affection. What should it be?

The guidebooks recommend postcards of home, but unless the hometown is Manhattan, Las Vegas or San Francisco—or Paris or Venice or London or Athens—chances are that the postcard will be filed in the wastebasket—and recycled, of course. Other forms of tribute can be paintings by one's children or small packs of candy. A more thoughtful visitor might take along a couple of those seductive full-color American seed catalogs to give a host at a commune; or *Science* or *Scientific American* or *National Geographic* or *The Smithsonian* magazines to bestow on a school; technical journals for a factory; or, for the daughter or son of the faithful escort who is also a young mother, a silly American T shirt or a satellite shot of Mars, or one of the astronauts' pictures of planet Earth showing the Great Wall; or a comic book; or a Polaroid snapshot of Mrs. Sun or Miss Chen at the head of her happy band of pilgrims. It's also a good idea to take along plenty of personal or professional calling cards; the Chinese are rather formal and appreciate such niceties.

There are some important caveats for the Foreign Friend:

However hot, stay cool. The Chinese are courteous and controlled; they regard a temper tantrum as the ultimate vulgarity. Any special request by the visitor (he wants to visit the university whereas the rest of the group is headed for a commune) can usually be met after temperate if prolonged discourse. The Responsible Person may start out with the catchall phrase "It is not convenient. . . ." But something can usually be arranged.

However irked, do not shirk. The day's schedule may not suit one's mood, but one is expected to stick with the group (except at rest times). Dropouts from the itinerary will mean loss of face for the hosts. However, if someone is sick or exhausted, the hosts will be sympathetic to the point of recommending acupuncture.

When in doubt, don't. No more than in Boston, Bonn or Bologna does one barge into someone's house in China without invitation—even though the houses are open to the street. Nor should one photograph people who obviously do not want their pictures taken. Carl Mydans recalls that in the 1940s most Chinese avoided being photographed because they believed that the camera captured the subject's soul as well as his image. While most people today willingly stand, sit or even ham for the photographer, some Chinese still resent the lens as an intrusion into privacy. Most other *Don'ts* are obvious. One does not discuss politics or ideologies unless the host initiates the conversation (which happens with surprising frequency), and even then with discretion. Guests at a banquet do not, during a host's speech or toast, exchange witticisms that they imagine to be incomprehensible to their hosts. Only barbarians speak in loud voice. Also: Be Punctual. The Chinese are.

In China, in short, one should tread, like King Agag, delicately.

The Arts:
From Clever to Sublime

"No other nation," an English scholar wrote of China, "has preserved its type so unaltered . . . developed a civilization so completely independent of any extraneous influences . . . elaborated its own ideals in such absolute segregation from alien thought." While this may never have been entirely true, the observation does help explain the millennia-long, self-sustaining vitality of the arts of the Middle Kingdom, a paradigm of expressiveness, adornment, form, function and technique.

Chinese art has always been *internally* eclectic, Ming painters, for example, drawing sedulously from the T'ang and Sung masters. Eclecticism has been carried to perverse extremes, as during the Cultural Revolution and the rule of the Gang of Four, when bullyboys ran amok, burning ancient paintings in the streets, closing art galleries, defacing ancient monuments; when old and foreign writings were proscribed, and living artists, authors, poets, composers and actors disgraced.

Today, the People's Republic is reaching strenuously backward, outward and forward. Backward to reclaim the once-suspect treasures of its past. Outward to embrace the arts, skills and techniques of the West. And forward to achieve a fusion of the best of both traditions.

Western symphony orchestras have been raptly received in mainland cities. Chinese orchestras are performing Bach, Beethoven, Mozart, Tchaikovsky, Liszt, Verdi, Puccini, Dvořák, Berlioz and other European masters. American folk songs are becoming familiar, even show tunes and rock 'n' roll. Chinese theatrical directors touring the United States have eagerly sought advice and books on lighting and staging techniques unknown to their own drama. Western authors have resurfaced in bookstores and libraries in China and are earnestly discussed. Theater and opera, reduced to repertoires of gaseous banality for more than a decade, have blossomed out with works that celebrate life and love rather than socialism and sweat. Love, an official pronouncement now allows, is "not wrong but necessary," a "part of social life and relations between people." More important, the word from Peking is that "art should be

120

subordinated to politics but not equated with politics." Says Chairman Hua: "Enlarge the repertoires of the performing arts."

Nowhere are the lively arts livelier. From the Peking opera, one of the oldest and most accomplished art forms on earth, to the local auditorium at Paotow in Inner Mongolia, audiences sit delighted through hours of drama and melodrama, comedy, orchestral music, chorales and solos, ballet, folk dance, mime, juggling, circus, puppetry and acrobatics—often combined in a single show. Not every troupe by any means is as polished as the chosen few that have toured Europe and North America, but the degree of proficiency, regardless of form or subject matter, is for the most part impressive and exhilarating.

Chinese acrobats are perhaps the deftest and most artistic on earth—or in air, which is where they mostly are while performing. In Kweilin's modern, air-conditioned theater of the Banyan Lake Hotel, the performers spin like dervishes and hurtle like hawks. A young man catches a stack of bowls on his head while riding a unicycle. A man and woman, secured by ribbons, whirl around a pole balanced on another man's chin, or mount a crazy pyramid of chairs with no visible means of support. Two bird-call imitators wind up their act with a scary mimicry of an air raid—flak, bombs, sirens and all (though neither artist could be old enough to have experienced one). Between acts a pair of stand-up comics do a fast-patter routine that would have wowed an Orpheum audience in the days of vaudeville.

Eclecticism invigorates Chinese music as well. Highlights of a recent concert in Shanghai: a pretty girl in a crimson shirt playing a dramatic ballad, "Five Martyrs of Wolf's Tooth Mountain," on the mandolinlike pipa; a superb xylophonist performing a Mongolian melody; a symphony orchestra playing excerpts from *Swan Lake,* introduced as "Lake of the Heavenly Goose." A big, brightly made-up baritone follows "Delivering Oil for the Motherland" with a German folksong in German. He is matched by a contralto in a white-pleated skirt singing "Kazak People Remember Chairman Mao" (the melody outshines the lyrics) and a French folk song in French. The audience munches sunflower seeds but does not converse loudly or move around during the performance.

At the auditorium in Paotow, a diminutive soprano belts out "Home on the Range"—in double time. An American audience responds with "Yankee Doodle" and "You Are My Sunshine." A Chinese guide volunteers "Jingle Bells"—in Chinese.

At sunrise on Shanghai's
Bund, crowds turn out
for balletic-athletic *t'ai
chi ch'uan.*

At a song and dance show in Canton's Sun Yat-sen
Memorial Hall, a striking building with a cavernous pillared
interior in traditional style, an excellent cellist plays a Kazak
folksong from Sinkiang province and a folk melody from
Hungary. Against a handsome backdrop of five rams (Canton is
sometimes called Five Ram City), eighteen accomplished
ballerinas perform *Flower Fair in Canton*, later followed by a
pretty peacock dance adapted from folk dances of Yunnan
province. In the meantime a baritone sings "Greeting Toast
When Friends from Foreign Countries Come" and "O Sole Mio."
There follows one of the few works with a tragic theme—an
orchestral suite, played with western instruments,
commemorating thwarted lovers who pine away and emerge
from their tombs as butterflies. The score, written in the 1950s
and until recently stricken from the repertory, echoes
Tchaikovsky, Khachaturian, Rimski-Korsakov and Armenian
folk melodies. A gifted young violinist plays Sarasate's
"Zigeunerweisen" and declines an encore. The evening's
principal set piece, in the style of classical Chinese opera,

Ping-Pong is serious, but
swimming on the Pearl
River is for fun; (over)
young acrobats of
Kwangsi Provincial
Troupe in action.

125

recounts in lively fashion the fable of an old scholar who rescues a wounded, wonderfully slavering wolf, which when recovered tries to devour the good man. The moral is sensible enough: *Do not show mercy to a dangerous animal.* In the finale, the ensemble does a folk dance to crashing music from Anhwei province with spectacular acrobatics.

There should be no shortage of artists in China's future. At schools like the Children's Palace in Shanghai's Yangpu district, talented children are selected at an early age to study the arts and, "in order to achieve modernization," the sciences. Officially, they must be in good health and well versed in the works of Mao (though this may swiftly change) as well as apt students. In ballet, singing, and instrumental and graphic art classes, children between the ages of eight and eleven demonstrate a remarkable precocity. In one chamber a well-tempered orchestra of eleven-year-olds, playing traditional Chinese dulcimers, mandolins, trumpets, fiddles, flutes, string drums and xylophone, perform enchantingly. In a nearby room, thirty-four young voices sing in chorus. No matter that the major opus is entitled "We Shall Become Commune Members When We Grow Up." (Not these gifted kids, one suspects.) Then, for the benefit of American friends, they break into "My Old Kentucky Home." Elsewhere, young ballerinas do everything short of *grands jetés* with aplomb. In the school auditorium, twenty-one young troupers perform an opera-ballet in praise of "fulfillment of tasks in a new historical period." (In all fairness, it should be remembered that the highly stylized Chinese dance theater is based not on literature but on action, playing and patterned charm.) When the Central Music Conservatory in Peking reopened after a long shutdown, 17,000 candidates applied for 130 places.

———————

More even than in the performing arts, the heavy hands of Mao and the Gang of Four still weigh down the graphic arts. "Art is no longer in a straitjacket," a Chinese critic observes, "but artists are." Remembering previous zigs and zags in cultural politics, the artists are—for the time being at least—understandably wary of innovation. Nothing approaching abstract art is to be seen in China. But they are now free at least to return to the classical themes of landscape—flora and fauna without any ideological content. It is doubtful that the authorities today would send to friendly countries anything like the collection of amateur peasant art from Shensi province that toured the United States in 1977. The eighty works, posterlike

The limestone peaks and
lambent waters of the Li
River Valley unfold like
a classic brush painting.

Nestled beside the Li River, the Yang Ti People's Commune overlooks lush fields and lotus ponds.

The rice crop is spread to dry (above); silkworm cocoons are sorted (below) and nurtured (top right) at Ho La People's Commune. Ducks waddle to market (below right).

Peasant girl sprays crops with insecticide at Ta Li People's Commune;
(below and right) Mrs. Ch'en Yen-liu and family do chores around the
house they own in Hao Mei village.

Mother and children take an outing in Wusih's Leave Your Pleasure Garden. (Below) An artisan in Soochow re-creates a traditional theme in silk. (Right) A needlepoint worker in Shanghai elaborates a new pattern.

Schoolchildren in Shanghai clap welcome to Foreign Friends.

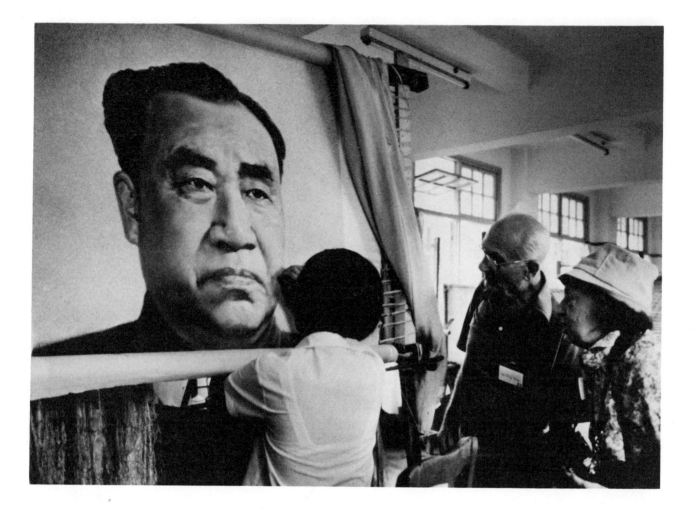

Artisan finishes silk-
thread portrait of
Marshal Chu Teh,
revolutionary leader.

paintings in candy-cane colors with such titles as "The New
Look of Our Piggery" and "Gathering a Bumper Crop of Cotton,"
were intended, according to the catalogue, to illustrate "the
abolition of the distinction between manual workers and brain
workers." They succeeded only too well.

Fiction and poetry too await a renaissance. However, a
number of distinguished writers denounced and banned as
"revisionist" during the Cultural Revolution have been
triumphantly restored to eminence. Among them is Pa Chin, in
his midseventies, who is best-known for a trilogy on the Chinese
family and is now translating the nineteent-century Russian
writer Aleksandr Herzen. More familiar to Americans is Lao
Sheh, author of *Ricksha Boy,* who has been posthumously
rehabilitated; he died in 1966 at the age of sixty-seven after
suffering verbal and physical castigation as an "active
counterrevolutionary."

The best bookstore in Kweilin advertises *The Book of
History,* a once-banned Confucian classic. Many western writers
condemned as "bourgeois" or worse are back on the shelves.

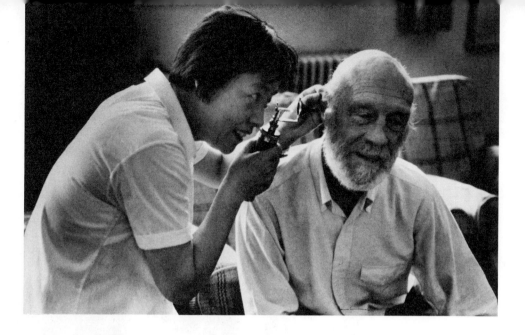

Gifted children play both
Western and Chinese
instruments; a "barefoot"
doctor learns the use of
otoscope from an American
physician; terra-cotta horse
and soldiers from the Chin
dynasty tomb near Sian.

Among them in English and translations: Walt Whitman,
Shakespeare, Faulkner, Steinbeck and Brecht. Visitors have seen
copies of Joseph Heller's *Catch-22* and Saul Bellow's novels. At a
reading of western poetry held in a Peking workers' gym, a
capacity audience of 20,000 sat intently while Shakespeare, the
Indian poet Rabindranath Tagore and "good" Russian writers
like Pushkin, Gorki and Mayakovski were read—some in
English—by poets and actors who had also been in limbo for a
dozen years.

While Mao was often caustically anti-intellectual and
deplored the age-old gulf between intelligentsia and peasant-
worker, many of his maxims have been adroitly excerpted to
justify this new ventilation of cultural life. "Let the past serve
the present," one of more famous dicta, now applies to the

Chinese tourists inspect their own Great Wall and Forbidden City.

restoration of the classics. His most celebrated *diktat*, "Let a hundred flowers bloom and a hundred schools of thought contend," though later repudiated, is once again an operative slogan. (In the Chairman's later years, a Peking intellectual notes ruefully, "there was one flower here, one flower there. But no blooms.")

Warning against further desecration of ancient treasures, Peking now emphasizes the difference between "appraisal of personages in history and the protection of historical relics." Which means, approximately, don't throw out the baby with the bathwater. Thus the mansion of Confucius in Shantung province, vandalized by Red Guards during Mao's anti-Confucian campaign, is now being restored. (Mao, something of a Confucianist himself, singled out the sage as a symbol of elitism and reverence for antiquity, therefore an antirevolutionary influence.) Historical hand-me-downs, Peking now argues sensibly enough, are "fruits of the labor of the people and should be preserved." Thus, no more defacing of monuments, no more burning of scrolls and, by extension, no more pillorying of honest artists.

To their credit, since the Communists came to power they have intensively explored, unearthed and assembled splendors that had been ignored during decades of civil and foreign wars. Many of these have been generously shared with the West in traveling exhibitions, most notably the prodigious array of 385 archeological treasures that toured Europe and North American in 1974. Some of the relics and hundreds of others are handsomely and intelligently displayed in three separate collections at Shanghai's Historical Museum.

The museum—it was a private bank before the Revolution— houses art and artifacts of every dynasty from the Shang, circa 1500 B.C., through the Ch'ing, ending in 1912. There are polished stone tools and rich Tang bronzes; iron wine-carafes shaped like elephants or horses; bronze vessels with motifs prefiguring Mayan ornamentation; chimes of bells to alert a nodding emperor; Ming celadons and cloisonné; pottery beakers and exquisite earthenware; ceremonial and burial objects of jade (once considered a sacred substance), ivory and turquoise; two terra-cotta soldiers and a snorting horse from the Emperor Shih-Huang's tomb near Sian. On the walls are monochrome, black-to-white paintings from the Tang, Sung and Ming dynasties, lyrical, contemplative celebrations of mighty landscape and little man, in which each brush stroke is a work of art in itself and the whole resonant of the quality that the Taoists called *ch'i-yun*, spiritual vitality. The museum has 250 professional staff members, half of whom are out in the field most of the time. Apparently, they were never forced to do their digging in people's communes.

————————

Walls do not a museum make, and China is an infinity of museums. There is hardly a single city without temples, pavilions, pagodas and gardens of surpassing grandeur, all wreathed in legend. Take Soochow, one of the most fascinating of all Chinese cities. . . . Just northwest of the city is Tiger Hill, so-called because a *Panthera tigris* is supposed to guard the tomb of the King of Wu, who made Soochow his capital. Interred with him, in the fifth century B.C., were a thousand workers who were sacrificed in order to keep his burial place secret. King He Lu was buried in The Sword Pool with 2,500 of his favorite blades. Atop Tiger Hill (it is more of a hillock) is a delicate seven-story pagoda, built in 961 B.C., that is China's answer to the Leaning Tower of Pisa; it has a 3¾-degree tilt.

The West Garden Temple in Soochow, built 400 years ago and rebuilt in 1898 after a fire, houses 500 larger-than-life figures of Buddha, smiling, scowling, scratching, blessing, musing and, in one instance, it seems, belching. Two or three of the more-powerful carvings transfix the barbarian's eye and appear to communicate with him.

In Soochow's aforementioned 450-year-old Humble Administrator's Garden, there are at least four pavilions as sublime as their names: Listening to The Rain on The Lotus Leaves, Thirty-Six Mandarin Duck, Moon Sighting, and Distant Perfumes.

Lion Forest Rock Garden, completed around 1350, boasts The Place Where One Questions The Plum Tree (it is said to be inscrutable). An even older *plaisanterie*, The Garden of The Pavilion of The Waves, built twelve years before the Norman Conquest of England, has pavilions of different periods in strikingly different styles, from Surging Waves to View of The Mountains to Hall of The Five Hundred Wise Men.

There is almost no end of pavilioned gardens in Soochow.... The 850-year-old Garden of The Fisherman's Retreat, the Sung-dynasty Garden of Joy, the more recent Garden of Harmony with its Pavilion of Stones Listening to The Lute.... Soochow is also noted for its beautiful women.

In contrast, most modern Chinese buildings, whether initiated from Peking or from Moscow during the ten-year Sino-Soviet dalliance, are severely functional, unadorned, drafty and deteriorating.

———————————

Chinese artisans nonetheless are still among the most skilled and painstaking craftsmen on earth. Their embroideries, silks, damasks, ceramics, porcelains, cloisonné, paper cuts, ivory and bamboo carvings; their jewelry of jade, gold, silver and ivory; their lacquerwork and wooden *objets*, fans of paper, silk, sandalwood and ivory, are all closer to art than craft. The ancient skills, one is told, have been revived and encouraged since the Revolution—and with good reason. Made almost entirely for export, the goods earn the People's Republic ample credit in foreign exchange.

They turn now to the westerner in friendship, spontaneously, without suspicion. They are, of course, amused and bemused by the varied shapes and sizes, clothes and colors of the strangers in their cities and villages. They are courteous and hospitable and proud. They are also healthy and handsome, as this portfolio shows. . . .

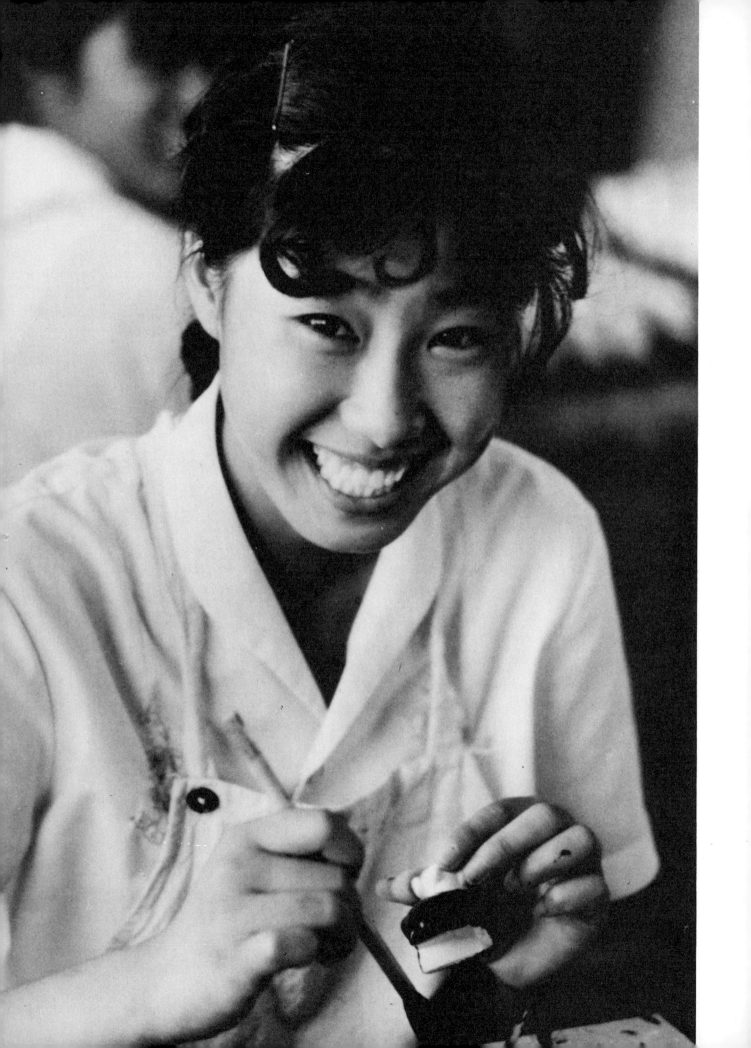

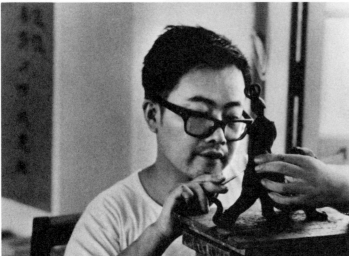

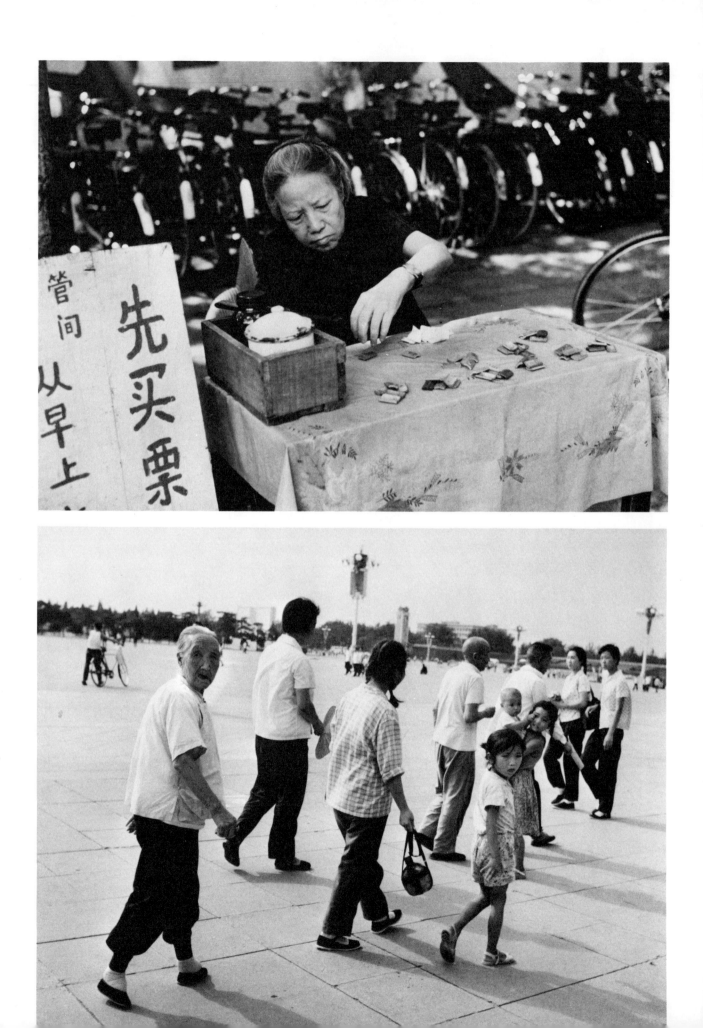

The old days still cast their shadows: on the worn face of a bicycle attendant in Wusih; on the bound feet of an old woman in Peking's T'ien An Men Square; on an overburdened mother in Canton.

Where Now? And How? And at What Cost?

We must make China rich and strong.
—WALL POSTER IN PEKING
JANUARY 1979

If there had been proletarian wall posters in nineteenth-century China, they would have said much the same thing. A hundred years ago China came to the belated conclusion that development of technology and science was essential to ensure China's "rightful place" in the world. But driven by internal conflict, invasion, occupation and foreign exploitation, the nation's leadership saw that goal perennially deferred until the 1949 Revolution. Then, in one remarkable decade, the peasant nation took huge strides forward in industrialization, agricultural output and modernization of a largely feudal society.

In the late 1950s the bold plans went into a stall. There was the utopian Great Leap Forward in 1958, in which farmers were expected to produce iron and steel in 700,000 backyard smelters. This scheme was an almost total failure. Agricultural and industrial production declined ominously. The surge of enthusiasm that had followed Liberation evaporated in factory and field. From the ancient imperial enclave in Peking, Chairman Mao Tse-tung railed against the West's preoccupation with productive efficiency, with its emphasis on material incentives; Mao feared that China, by following suit, would create a new elite of technocrats and bureaucrats. The economy was dealt a more punishing blow in 1960 when 1,400 Russian technicians pulled out, leaving a shambles of unfinished factories ad abandoned targets.

There ensued a decade of disaster—the Great Proletarian Cultural Revolution, followed by the rule of the Gang of Four—in which the nation virtually ground to a standstill in the name of ideological purity. Still, a few moderates such as Premier Chou En-lai never lost sight of the need for "modernization," with all that it implied: most notably a new era of friendship with Western Europe and such old opponents as Japan and the United States. Among those who shared his views were China's present-day leaders, Chairman Hua Kuo-feng and Senior Vice Premier Teng Hsiao-p'ing. Even Mao in his physical and political decline seems to have come around to their view. In his last interview with Mao, Edgar Snow, the distinguished American journalist and longtime friend of the Chairman, quoted him as saying that "he would place his hopes on the American people." In fact, after the near-fatal embrace of the Russian bear, China's leaders determined never again to depend on a single foreign partner.

By the time of the Eleventh Party Congress in August 1977, the nation was ready for its Great Leap Outward. Mao was dead; the Gang of Four had been ousted; Hua and Teng were in power. The people, rueful and somber, appeared eager to work for a technological revolution on as vast a scale as the political upheaval that had created their Republic. China formally embarked on the Four Modernizations, aimed at bringing industry, agriculture, science and technology, and defense into line with those of the advanced nations by the year 2000. It is a staggeringly ambitious undertaking, by far the biggest ever attempted in so short a term. By fairly conservative estimates, it may cost at least $600 billion.

Tough-minded Chinese teams bustled around the world in search of expertise, credits and hardware. The hermetic People's Republic began opening up to foreigners. Businessmen swarmed into the country like bees in a clover patch. The American tourist became immediately aware of the new attitude, from officialdom to the lowliest commune. He was made welcome— not only because of the hard currency his presence might generate but also in a subtler way. Even before the restoration of diplomatic relations with the United States, the American visitor felt a tingle of excitement quite unlike the sensation aroused by a first encounter with, say, chilly Russia. There was the exhilaration of a first date or, for some, the warmth of an old love regained.

It is possible that the courtship promises too much too fast. Few westerners profess to understand China; the Chinese do not always appear to understand themselves. There is a strong suspicion among some Americans—and most Russians—that the Chinese are using the American connection mainly for geopolitical and psychological reasons, as a lever against Soviet encirclement or hegemony—pa-chu'an, literally, "overbearing power." Certainly, despite clear signals of its intentions, China's new friends were dismayed and perplexed by its punitive strike

From all over the world come the materials and technology for modernization. (Next page) Sun bursts through cloud over a steel mill on the Yangtze River.

against Vietnam in 1979, with all the attendant risks of Soviet military retaliation or at least an accelerated contest for influence in Southeast Asia. That or any other classic guns-versus-butter dilemma, if protracted, might force the Chinese to choose tanks over automobiles, gunpowder rather than pork chops, after all.

Now, however, it may not be so easy to reverse the engines. There are great internal pressures on the regime to raise living standards and protect the citizenry from bureaucratic oppression. Peking in 1979 was faced with the unprecedented spectacle, in a Socialist society, of ragged peasants pouring in from every single province to demand a better deal. The Letters-to-the-Editor column in *People's Daily*, revived after years in limbo, reportedly receives some 50,000 missives a month, mostly irate. When readers protested increases in the cost of vegetables, the prices were swiftly lowered. Other readers have reported instances of shady deals by bosses. Many plead with their leaders

to restore and uphold "Socialist legality." Wall posters have called for a greater degree of "democracy" and protection of "human rights."

Overtly, at least, the government seems to be responsive to such demands. It seems particularly concerned—as was Mao—about the rigid, inflated and often arbitrary bureaucracy. (China has an estimated 20 million civil servants.)

People's Daily has conceded: "The facts show that a number of leading cadres are not accustomed to respecting and protecting the democratic rights of the masses. . . . If the people could not vent their views on state affairs and criticize party and government functionaries, including leaders, would not all this talk about socialist democracy be empty talk?" *People's Daily* has invoked Karl Marx's observation "I know only that I am not a Marxist," to make the point that Maoism-Marxism "is a philosophy, not a religious dogma." The party organ added: "Let the people say what they will, the heavens will not fall."

Beyond words, a new constitution adopted in March 1978 pledges greater freedom of expression for individuals and for the arts and a more democratic legal system with public trials and the defendant's right to have counsel (though China is extremely short of trained lawyers). China's leaders do apparently have a real fear that their country may wind up, like the Soviet Union, with a massive, self-perpetuating managerial class with all the material perquisites of their capitalist counterparts.

There is a real danger, of course, that in their drive for modernization the Chinese may actually create a super-elite. How, for instance, will the thousands of their ablest young people who study abroad view their authoritarian society on their return? How will they be treated? For all their resistance to things "un-Chinese," can *K'o-k'ou-K'o-le* ("Tastes Good, Tastes Happy"), disco dancing, modern hotels and the coming mini-army of western technicians fail to affect their sternly puritanical society? Can Sparta remain immune to Athens? For, whatever its ambitions, China today is still one of the most tightly regimented societies on earth, its people subject to direction from preconception to death, controlled in everything they may learn, wear, eat, read, see or do for a living or for pleasure.

Under the present leadership, given its goals of modernization, China's compass is almost certainly tilted toward a more democratic society. There are disquieting questions, however. There are rumors of strains within the Politburo. Could there be another schism? If the aging Teng were to die, would his liberalizing influence be effaced? Can China actually afford its grandiose new programs? (Some western economists doubt it.) Were Sino-Soviet hostilities to intensify, as well they might, would China have to divert even more than the ill-spared 8 percent of its GNP that now goes to defense? Can the communes continue to nourish the ever-growing population? How severely would two or three bad growing seasons crimp the economy? Suppose the vast, unplumbed offshore oil reserves turn out to be a South Sea Bubble?

There is a cryptic Confucian proverb to the effect that one cannot boil an egg in a teapot. One can take this to mean that it is impractical if not presumptuous to compress large problems within a small space, whether of time or of type.

The rest of the civilized world can only hope, as do many thoughtful Chinese, that the People's Republic will succeed in its headlong drive to become a modern nation, and that it will achieve an equable, prosperous, peaceful and stable society. If it fails, we shall not have heard the last thunder out of China.